Career Launcher

Health Care Providers

Career Launcher series

Career Launcher

Health Care Providers

Sheila Buff

Ferguson Publishing
An imprint of Infobase Publishing

Career Launcher: **Health Care Providers**

Copyright © 2010 by Infobase Publishing, Inc.

Ferguson
An imprint of Infobase Publishing
132 West 31st Street
New York NY 10001

Library of Congress Cataloging-in-Publication Data

Buff, Sheila.
    Health care providers / by Sheila Buff.
       p. cm. — (Career launcher)
    Includes bibliographical references and index.
    ISBN-13: 978-0-8160-7954-4 (hardcover : alk. paper)
    ISBN-10: 0-8160-7954-4 (hardcover : alk. paper) 1. Allied health person-nel—Vocational guidance—United States—Popular works. 2. Public health personnel—Vocational guidance—United States—Popular works. 3. Medical personnel—Vocational guidance—United States—Popular works. I. Title.
    R697.A4B84 2010
    610.69023—dc22

                                                  2009049667

You can find Ferguson on the World Wide Web at http://www.fergpubco.com

Produced by Print Matters, Inc.
Text design by A Good Thing, Inc.
Cover design by Takeshi Takahashi
Cover printed by Art Print Company, Taylor, PA
Book printed and bound by Maple Press, York, PA
Dated printed: May 2010

Printed in the United States of America

10 9 8 7 6 5 4 3 2 1

This book is printed on acid-free paper.

Contents

Foreword

My career in health care began when I was only 16. I worked as an orderly in a small community hospital, doing all sorts of things: I helped with patient personal care, patient transport, and cleaning rooms. By the time I was 19, I was a registered nurse with an associate's degree. My early nursing jobs took me to a lot of different settings: emergency room care, critical care, cardiac step-down unit, and general medical and surgical nursing.

Working in so many different settings taught me a lot in a hurry—and it also made me realize that I needed more education if I was going to advance to a leadership position in nursing. I went for my bachelor's degree while working full time, which was not easy. It paid off when I was promoted to a clinical supervisor position in a big hospital. Because nurses are also teachers, my career eventually took me into nursing education, first as an instructor and eventually as the director of the School of Nursing at Western Carolina University. I now supervise the work of 32 faculty members and between 350 and 400 students every year. In my years of hospital work and with the School of Nursing, I have seen many nurses and other health care professionals go on to highly successful careers. Several factors make these individuals stand out to me and to their employers.

The most successful health care professionals I know have a high level of emotional maturity. These people are able to feel empathy for their patients, but also handle difficult patients without losing their cool. They are flexible in the workplace, especially in acute care settings, emergency rooms, and other places where the situation can change rapidly. They can roll with the changes and stay calm and effective.

Emotional maturity also lets you see the bigger picture and understand the context of management decisions. It is important to see beyond the narrow view from your particular unit or clinical area. Do not get mired in the day-to-day work—try to grasp the larger mission.

I have found that emotional maturity does not have a lot to do with age—some twenty-year-olds are more mature than people many years older than them. On the other hand, I have also found that older students who return to school bring a high level of seriousness and purpose to their studies. They are able to apply their life and work experience to their health care careers and often do very well once they start working.

Another important aspect of success in health care is being engaged with the organization, be it a hospital, clinic, doctors' office, nursing home, or outpatient center. The health care professionals who move on to leadership roles participate actively in policy committees, quality improvement programs, and other work that supports and advances the organization—and supports and advances their careers as well.

One of the most admirable traits I have noticed in my most successful students is a strong desire for more education. These people have developed a pattern of embracing learning that goes beyond just continuing education requirements and in-service training. They want to stay on the cutting edge of their profession. They enjoy the challenge of going on for additional degrees and certifications and know that the knowledge they gain will help them help their patients. It is not always easy to go to classes after a long shift, but successful health care professionals do it anyway.

Education is also key to moving forward with your health care career. Certification exams are a great way to do this. The exams are challenging and take a lot of study and clinical work. By passing them, you receive recognition for your excellent skills and experience. Certifications let you climb the clinical career ladder without having to move into management. You get recognized without having to stop doing what you love—working with patients.

Another crucial aspect of success in health care is good interpersonal communications. Today, health care workers are part of a team. You need to work collaboratively with the other team members to solve problems, brainstorm, and provide the best care for your patients. The old-fashioned hierarchy, where doctors give orders to nurses who give orders to those below them, does not apply any longer. Other professionals, such as respiratory therapists and social workers, are crucial and equal members of the health care team. The input of everyone on the team, including patient aides and even the people who clean patient rooms, can be helpful. A respectful attitude toward everyone on the team is vital for moving your career forward. There can be multiple pathways to a good outcome for your patients. Recognizing this, and being flexible, respectful, and cooperative, makes it easier to work with your team members and make sure your patients get the care they need.

Good communications are always respectful and courteous. Unfortunately, sometimes people forget that e-mails, social networking sites, and other media can reflect on their professional life. I have seen some promising careers be derailed by indiscreet e-mails, phone messages, and inappropriate Web site postings. As a health care professional entrusted with a lot of responsibility, your basic integrity is important, even when you are off duty.

Despite all the training and work they put in to get their certifications and degrees, many health care workers end up leaving the field within three to five years. Sometimes this is because they discover they really just do not like the work, even though their clinical training gave them a good idea of what to expect. Others find that shift work, especially night shifts, is too disruptive.

As a health educator, the dropout issue concerns me deeply. We put a lot of effort and expense into training health care workers. We want them to be happy in their work and remain as productive members of the workforce, especially at a time when there is a serious shortage of health care personnel.

How can health care workers avoid burnout and disillusionment with their jobs? There is no magic solution, but I know from my former students who have gone on to long and successful careers that choosing your first employer carefully is a major factor. Your first year in health care is really a sort of internship, where you take what you have learned in the classroom and in your clinical training and start to put it to use. This is a very challenging time. You have new levels of responsibility that you might not feel quite ready for. We know that how well you are mentored during this crucial first year will make a big difference in how you feel about your career. New workers who get the support they need are much more likely to stay and succeed in health care.

In many health care professions, such as nursing and physical therapy, new graduates are assigned a preceptor—someone who is there to guide them through that first year. In most cases, this a formal relationship. Ideally, you will meet regularly with your preceptor to discuss your progress and any issues you feel you need help with, and your preceptor will also be available to advise you at other times. In other areas of health care, you might not have a formal preceptor, but you will probably have someone in the department who will be asked to act as a mentor to you, helping you learn the ropes and adjust to your new job. No matter what the relationship is called, if it is a good one it will help you learn a lot, make a good adjustment to the demands of the working world, and enjoy your work. A poor relationship, however, can be so frustrating that you might drop out of health care. If you feel your preceptor or mentor is not giving you the support you need, discuss the issue with your supervisor.

In addition to your formal or informal mentoring, draw on the skills and experience of the people around you. If you are uncertain about what to do, if you need assistance, if you are asked to do something you do not feel you understand, ask for help. Be willing to learn from anyone, no matter what their job description.

To be sure your early jobs are a good learning experience for you, and that you will be mentored well, look for a position in a magnet hospital. When a hospital earns the magnet designation, it means that it strongly supports the nursing staff, provides a healthy workplace, believes in evidence-based medicine, and is deeply concerned with staff satisfaction. When a hospital follows magnet concepts, it benefits everyone on the staff, not just the nurses. A magnet hospital, or any work setting that supports magnet concepts, will be a great starting point to begin or advance your career.

During the hiring process, interview the employer just as much as the hiring manager and others interview you. You want to know that your skills and interests are a good fit for the job. You also want to know that the benefits, such as reimbursement and time off for continuing education, meet industry standards. Most importantly, both you and the employer need to agree that your first six to 12 months on the job are an orientation period. During that time, you want to be sure you will get the mentoring and training you need to learn your job and do the best you can for your patients.

The responsibility for getting through your first years on the job is not just with your employer. This is a very stressful period for you. Learning to handle the stress will not only help you survive and thrive, it will give you lifelong coping skills. From my experience and that of my colleagues and students, I strongly suggest that all health care workers make very effort to have a satisfying life outside of their work. Have strong interests in other areas. Make time for your family and friends. Most important, do not neglect yourself. Get enough rest. Chronic sleep deprivation from shift work and overtime is a serious problem in the health care workplace. It leads to errors, and it is bad for your physical and mental health. Be good to yourself. Eat a healthy diet, get some exercise, and make time for your needs.

Health care jobs today are already challenging. Patients in hospitals and nursing homes are sicker than ever and their care is increasingly complex, involving many skills and specialties. Patients with chronic diseases who were once hospitalized or in skilled nursing facilities are now often cared for at home; treatment that was once given in a hospital setting is now provided in outpatient clinics or through home care. Your ongoing success in the changing health care environment will depend on being flexible, adaptable, and willing to learn.

—Vincent P. Hall, Ph.D., R.N., C.N.E.
DIRECTOR, SCHOOL OF NURSING,
WESTERN CAROLINA UNIVERSITY

Acknowledgments

Many, many health care professionals generously answered my questions and pointed me in the right directions for this book. They are too numerous to name—but they know who they are and they know how grateful I am. I'd also like to thank Chuck Curlee, R.R.T., C.R.T.T., Susan Racemi, R.N., and Lara Simmons, M.S., for allowing me to interview them. Vincent P. Hall, Ph.D., R.N., C.N.E., Director, School of Nursing, Western Carolina University contributed a wonderful foreword based on his long personal experience with both nursing and nurse education. Thanks also go to Associate Dean Regis M. Gilman, Ed.D., who put me in touch with Dr. Hall. Western Carolina University is fortunate to have such dedicated administrators. Richard Rothschild of Print Matters brought me on for this book, and David Andrews provided a sure editorial hand. Finally, thanks to Joe and Dina for always being there.

Introduction

Health care today is one of the most rapidly growing areas of employment in the country. In 2009, more than 14 million people worked in health care nationwide, and that number is projected to grow by some 3 million more jobs by 2016. Because the American population is aging and needs more health care both now and well into the future, the demand for health care workers is high and getting stronger. In addition, access to health care is improving, meaning that more people overall will be able to get the health care they need. The current demands on the health care system have already led to shortages of registered nurses and other health care workers—demand in the future will lead to even more job openings for qualified workers. If you have a desire to help people and are willing to work hard at a challenging and satisfying career with room for advancement, health care could be your future.

The range of jobs in health care is very wide. People interested in entering the field have many options, ranging from professional-level jobs requiring extensive training to jobs that are easier to enter but still offer opportunities for advancement. The purpose of this book is to help you understand the large and complex world of health care, find a role that suits your interests and abilities, and then help you to succeed and advance in your health care career.

This book focuses on the allied health professions—the many skilled workers who assist doctors, dentists, and other professionals in providing quality health care to patients. Today about 60 percent of all the workers in health care are in the allied health professions. They are an essential part of the medical team that treats patients throughout their illness. Working under the supervision of doctors and others, they provide a great deal of the hands-on health care that patients receive. Generally speaking, the allied health professions are grouped into three main areas:

➧ Associated health care workers. These workers provide nursing care and other types of care directly to patients. They work very closely with doctors and have a high level of training. This group of workers includes registered nurses, nurse practitioners, licensed practical nurses, physician assistants, and dietitians and nutritionists.

➜ Adjunctive health care workers. Adjunctive health care workers are generally technologists, technicians, assistants, and aides who have been trained in a particular skill. This is a very large area that includes most jobs in allied health care outside of nursing. Some adjunctive health care workers operate complex equipment such as CT scanners, diagnostic ultrasound machines, equipment that tests heart function, dialysis machines that keep people with kidney failure alive, and the nuclear medicine machinery used to give radiation therapy. EMTs and paramedics provide first-line emergency care. Other adjunctive health care workers include laboratory technicians, pharmacy technicians, surgical technologists, nurse's aides, and medical assistants. Health educators bring health and wellness information to patients and the public. Dentistry is also a major area for adjunctive health care workers such as dental hygienists and dental assistants.

➜ Rehabilitation health care workers. Most rehabilitation workers are therapists of various sorts. They are trained professionals who help patients recover from health problems that can affect their normal function and help people with disabilities maintain and improve their normal functioning. Workers in this area include physical therapists, respiratory therapists, occupational therapists, speech-language pathologists, and health educators. In many therapy areas assistants and aides work with the therapists to help treat patients. Home health aides work with patients who have chronic illnesses or disabilities. They provide health care in the home and allow these patients to stay out of the hospital and remain as independent as possible. Today the demand for home health care workers is very high—this is the fastest-growing area in all of health care.

In addition to allied health care workers who provide care directly to patients, the health care system relies heavily on administrative workers who handle the vast amounts of recordkeeping, billing, and other paperwork that patient care creates. This important area includes medical coders, health information technologists, and medical transcriptionists.

Allied health care workers are found just about every place health care is delivered. They work in hospitals, rehabilitation centers, nursing homes, outpatient clinics, dialysis centers, imaging centers, in doctors' and dentists' offices, and in patients' homes. Health care workers can often choose the work setting that fits their skills and schedules best.

Helping You Decide

Which of these many possible health care professions is right for you? Helping you choose the right area is a key goal of this book, whether you are deciding on how to continue your education, are already studying for a career in health care, and even if you are already working in the industry.

To help you understand how the health care industry has grown and changed, especially in recent years, first read through the brief history of health care in chapter 1, Industry History. You will get an idea of the long history of compassionate care and how it has evolved into the many specialized areas of modern medicine. You will learn how the allied health care professions have become increasingly important in recent decades and how advances in medicine have led to new career paths.

In chapter 2, State of the Industry, you will get a thorough look at where the health care industry is today—and where it is headed. You will learn that most health care jobs are among the highest paying and most secure of any industry in the country. You will also learn that demand for health care workers in every field today is very high—and in most cases, growing rapidly as well. This chapter is based on detailed information and statistics from professional societies, industry sources, and government statistics. All sources agree: The future for health care workers is bright.

In chapter 3, On the Job, you will get an in-depth look at the most important allied health care careers—in all, this chapter includes 41 job descriptions. For each job title—respiratory therapy technician, for example—you will get a detailed explanation of the job, including:

➜ What sort of training is needed
➜ What the employment outlook is
➜ What you can expect to do each day

➡ The range of typical salaries and hourly wages
➡ What the opportunities for advancement are

This chapter focuses on the most common allied health careers, ranging from those that require an advanced degree (physical therapist or nurse practitioner, for example) to those that people with a high school degree or the equivalent can enter (home health care aide or certified nursing assistant). The goal of this chapter is to help you find allied health careers that match your interests, your level of education, and your commitment to further training. The information is based on the most recent government and industry statistics and is as accurate and up-to-date as possible.

Bear in mind that in health care, where you start is not where you have to end, and that ongoing education is part of the job. The training and experience you gain as a home health care aide, for example, can be the starting point for going on to become a licensed practical or vocational nurse; from there, your career could take you on to becoming a registered nurse. Does this take a lot of hard work? Yes. It is not easy to work and also take classes, but the payoff in terms of better pay and greater career opportunities makes it worthwhile.

Chapter 4, Tips for Success, gives you the inside information you need to move your career forward. This chapter includes detailed advice on choosing a good training program that meets state and industry requirements and finding ways to pay for it. The chapter also includes solid information on meeting continuing education requirements and going on to higher levels of education. Tips for finding your first job in health care, planning your career, and moving up to higher levels of training and responsibility are also found here, along with advice on being professional and coping with the stresses and problems of health care work. Because certification and licensing requirements are extremely important for health care workers, this chapter explains these crucial concepts in depth.

Health care is full of specialized and complex vocabulary, abbreviations, acronyms, jargon, and shorthand expressions. In chapter 5, Talk Like a Pro, you will find a glossary of useful terms to help you sort out the language of health care.

Finally, chapter 6, Resources, looks at the many accrediting and certifying agencies and professional organizations that set the standards for allied health care workers and educational institutions.

They provide information, job leads, industry news, continuing education, and other services to their members. These organizations are a great source of additional information for anyone considering a career in a particular health care area. This chapter also includes a list of reliable Web sites for finding medical information and an extensive list of books that help you get a real feel for what health care is all about.

Chapter 1

Industry History

Health care workers today are part of a long healing tradition that dates to the dawn of human history. From shamanism to robotic surgery, healing through skilled and compassionate care has always been the goal.

Medicine as a true profession dates back to Hippocrates, who was born in ancient Greece around 460 B.C.E. Often called the father of modern medicine, Hippocrates carefully studied the human body and its diseases, drawing on centuries of Greek medical tradition before him. Hippocrates and his followers were the first to describe many diseases, especially those of the lungs and chest, and were the first to systematically describe the phases of an illness, using terms such as acute, chronic, relapse, and convalescence—concepts that are still used today. On the other hand, Hippocrates believed that all illness was caused by an imbalance in the humors of the body. When these mysterious fluids—blood, black bile, yellow bile, and phlegm—were out of balance, illness followed. Restoring the balance of the humors would cure the patient. One way to rebalance the humors was to bleed the patient. The four humors concept has no basis in reality, yet because Hippocrates believed it, and because he was held in such high esteem by later generations of physicians, the idea continued well into the 19th century.

Hippocrates set medicine apart as a profession. He observed his patients carefully, took vital signs such as the pulse and respiration rate, and kept written records that could be passed on to other physicians. Hippocrates also created the Hippocratic oath, a statement of professional ethics. The original oath has been modified quite a bit, but it serves as the standard for similar oaths taken by many medical professionals as they begin their careers. They all vow to follow good medical practices, uphold a high moral standard, and above all, avoid harming their patients.

Hippocrates was such a powerful influence that for centuries his work was accepted without question. It was not until the second century c.e. that Galen, a Roman physician of Greek origin, moved medicine forward with studies of anatomy, systematic observations of patients, and new ideas in surgery. Roman medicine before and after Galen was fairly sophisticated—medical devices such as the scalpel were invented during this time. After the fall of the Roman Empire, however, much medical knowledge was lost. For centuries, medical advances were almost nonexistent as doctors continued to slavishly follow Hippocrates and Galen. At the same time, however, traditional healing, practiced mostly by women, also continued. These healers treated common health problems and injuries with herbs and assisted with childbirth.

In the Middle Ages, what medical care there was for serious illness came from the men and women of religious orders. They began the first hospitals, places where medical care, usually for the poor, was provided by someone other than the patient's family. The word hospital comes from the Latin word *hospes*, meaning host. (The English words hotel and hostel also come from this root.) The medical care was primitive, but the concept of the hospital as a place where sick people received compassionate care paid for by charity became well established. To this day, almost all hospitals in the United States are nonprofit organizations; many were founded by religious groups and still maintain that affiliation.

Scientific medicine gradually stirred to life again starting in the 1400s. In the 16th century, Andreas Vesalius (1514–1564) began his studies of the human body. The founder of modern human anatomy, Vesalius made many important discoveries based on his dissections of human bodies (mostly condemned criminals). He dared to show that Galen was often wrong in his descriptions of body parts. Among other crucial discoveries, Vesalius showed that the heart has four chambers and created highly detailed drawings of the muscles of the body. Vesalius' work was important not only for his discoveries but for his willingness to go beyond Hippocrates and Galen. His work looked forward to the future, not back to the past.

Everyone
Knows

The Hippocratic Oath: Modern Version

I swear to fulfill, to the best of my ability and judgment, this covenant:

I will respect the hard-won scientific gains of those physicians in whose steps I walk, and gladly share such knowledge as is mine with those who are to follow.

I will apply, for the benefit of the sick, all measures [that] are required, avoiding those twin traps of overtreatment and therapeutic nihilism.

I will remember that there is art to medicine as well as science, and that warmth, sympathy, and understanding may outweigh the surgeon's knife or the chemist's drug.

I will not be ashamed to say "I know not," nor will I fail to call in my colleagues when the skills of another are needed for a patient's recovery.

I will respect the privacy of my patients, for their problems are not disclosed to me that the world may know. Most especially must I tread with care in matters of life and death. If it is given me to save a life, all thanks. But it may also be within my power to take a life; this awesome responsibility must be faced with great humbleness and awareness of my own frailty. Above all, I must not play at God.

I will remember that I do not treat a fever chart, a cancerous growth, but a sick human being, whose illness may affect the person's family and economic stability. My responsibility includes these related problems, if I am to care adequately for the sick.

I will prevent disease whenever I can, for prevention is preferable to cure.

I will remember that I remain a member of society, with special obligations to all my fellow human beings, those sound of mind and body as well as the infirm.

If I do not violate this oath, may I enjoy life and art, respected while I live and remembered with affection thereafter. May I always act so as to preserve the finest traditions of my calling and may I long experience the joy of healing those who seek my help.

(Written in 1964 by Louis Lasagna, Academic Dean of the School of Medicine at Tufts University, and used in many medical schools today.)

The pace of medical discovery began to move much more quickly after Vesalius showed the way. The English physician, William Harvey, for example, discovered the circulation of the blood in the mid-1600s. Despite all the discoveries, however, doctors continued to believe that disease was caused by imbalanced humors. They had no idea that germs caused illness, and of course had no idea that dirty hands and impure water transmitted disease.

The Birth of Modern Nursing

During the Revolutionary War, makeshift hospitals treated wounded soldiers, and temporary hospitals were often opened by city authorities during epidemics. By the late 1700s, the idea of a hospital had begun to change from a religious institution to a secular one. Medical hospitals staffed by physicians and surgeons, assisted by nurses, began to appear. The earliest American hospitals in this sense were Pennsylvania General Hospital in Philadelphia, which opened in 1751, New York Hospital, which opened in 1771, and Massachusetts General Hospital, a latecomer in 1821. Still, hospitals were seen as places only for the very poor or for people who had no family to care for them. The first hospitals for women were founded by female doctors in this period: The New York Infirmary for Women and Children in New York City in 1860 and the New England Hospital for Women and Children in Boston in 1862. African-Americans founded Provident Hospital in Chicago in 1893 and Douglass Hospital in Philadelphia in 1895. Hospitals also began to offer outpatient clinics, often the only access the urban poor had to health care.

Modern medicine truly begins in the 19th century, when scientific advances by Joseph Lister, Louis Pasteur, and Robert Koch led to the germ theory and antiseptic surgery. Death rates from infectious diseases and from infection following surgery and childbirth dropped dramatically as the century went on. The hospital system in Europe and America expanded greatly in the 19th century. In addition to nonprofit hospitals sponsored by religious denominations, major cities such as New York, Boston, and Chicago opened large public hospitals, spurred on by rapid increases in population and the lessons about large-scale hospitals learned in the Civil War. As formal medical schools became established as divisions of universities, they opened research hospitals. The need for hospitals grew in the 19th century along with population, especially in urban areas.

By 1900, there were about 1,400 hospitals in the United States. Hospitals began to provide specialized treatment—for eye problems or tuberculosis, for example. By the 1920s, that number had grown to more than 6,000. By 1935, a third of all Americans were born in or died in a hospital.

The 19th century also saw the birth of nursing as a profession. Women had always been active in health care as nurses and midwives, but it was not until Florence Nightingale (1820–1910) brought hygiene and good nutrition to wounded British soldiers in the Crimean War in the 1850s that the value of trained nurses began to be appreciated. Nightingale was born into a wealthy and cultured English family. At the age of 25, she announced her desire to go into nursing. Her decision created fierce opposition in her family—women of her class were expected to become wives and mothers, and careers were out of the question. Nightingale overcame her family's objections, however, and trained in Germany, where nursing as a profession was taken seriously. On her return to England, she began working for improved medical care for the poor at free clinics and in workhouses.

Nightingale achieved international fame through her work in the Crimean War. Conditions for the British wounded were horrible and the death rate in military hospitals in Turkey was extremely high. In 1854, Nightingale and 38 women volunteer nurses, all trained by her, arrived at the main military hospital in Scutari in Turkey. They found that medicines and other supplies were very scarce, hygiene was nonexistent, and infections were rampant. Nightingale's first task was to convince the overworked, indifferent doctors and medical staff that something needed to be done at all. Once she and her nurses got to work cleaning the hospitals, improving the defective sewers, and bringing ventilation, nutritious food, and good nursing care to the soldiers, the death rate dropped rapidly. Within six months of her arrival, the mortality rate went from 42 percent to 2.2 percent. Nightingale's observations linking good sanitary conditions with good healing were crucial for the future design of hospitals and for the home care of the sick.

Nightingale returned home from the Crimean War and soon became sick with an unidentified ailment that kept her confined to her bed for much of the rest of her long life. Even so, her fierce energy remained and she stayed extremely active and influential, working constantly to make nursing a serious profession based on modern ideas and scientific knowledge. In 1860, she created the Nightingale Training School at St. Thomas' Hospital in London, which exists today as the Florence Nightingale School of Nursing and Midwifery. Also in 1860, Nightingale published *Notes on Nursing: What It Is and What It Is Not*, a no-nonsense volume that was the basis of the curriculum at the Nightingale School. It was also a popular bestseller of its time. To this day, despite its old-fashioned language and assumption that all nurses are women, it is considered a classic introduction to the art and science of nursing.

Nightingale's work inspired nurses during the Civil War. As they had in the Crimea, her ideas about sanitation met with strong resistance from Union military doctors, but they inspired the all-volunteer U.S. Sanitary Commission. The Commission set up field hospitals for the Union wounded following Nightingale's principles, helping to save the lives of many soldiers.

For the rest of her life, Nightingale worked tirelessly to improve nursing training and practice and to improve medical care for the military and the poor. The pivotal importance of her work cannot be overemphasized. To this day, nursing graduates take the Nightingale Pledge, a modified version of the Hippocratic Oath that was composed in 1893 by Mrs. Lystra E. Gretter and a Committee for the Farrand Training School for Nurses in Detroit. It reads,

> I solemnly pledge myself before God and in the presence of this assembly, to pass my life in purity and to practice my profession faithfully.
> I will abstain from whatever is deleterious and mischievous, and will not take or knowingly administer any harmful drug. I will do all in my power to maintain and elevate the standard of my profession, and will hold in confidence all personal matters committed to my keeping and all family affairs coming to my knowledge in the practice of my calling.

During the Civil War, nurses such as Dorothea Dix (1802–1887) and Clara Barton (1821–1912) saved the lives of countless soldiers. Their contributions did for American nurses what Florence Nightingale had done in England. Dorothea Dix went on to play a major role in improving care for mental patients. Clara Barton went on to found the American Red Cross, an organization that today plays an essential role in disaster relief and provides about half of the American blood supply.

The life of a nurse in the late 1800s was far from easy. Here is how Linda Richards, who became America's first professionally trained nurse, described her education: "We rose at 5.30 A.M. and left the wards at 9 P.M. to go to our beds, which were in little rooms between the wards. Each nurse took care of her ward of six patients both day and night. Many a time I got up nine times in the night; often I did not get to sleep before the next call came. We had no evenings out, and no hours for study or recreation. Every second week we were off duty one afternoon from two to five o'clock. No monthly allowance was given for three months."

Once training was over, a typical workday began at 7 A.M. and continued to 8 P.M., seven days a week, for a salary of $30 a month. After five years of steady work, a nurse could expect a raise of five cents a day. On the other hand, nursing was one of the few professions open to women (the other major option was teaching), and

Problem Solving

Attracting the Best Staff

With demand for allied health care workers at an all-time high, and with a serious nursing shortage, how can hospitals and other health organizations attract and keep the best talent? It is not easy. Most experts agree that health care workers are most attracted to a setting where their skills are not only respected but where they have opportunities to improve those skills and feel their work is truly helping patients. In fact, studies show that other factors, such as pay and shift work, are usually less important to health care workers. A major reason behind high turnover rates among health care workers is badly defined and constantly changing job expectations. Another reason is inadequate training. When workers are asked to do things they feel are beyond their capacity, they may do a poor job and even harm a patient. Poor training also leads to on-the-job injuries, one of the major reasons health care workers leave the profession altogether. Clear professional standards, ongoing training, mentoring, and good management can go a long way toward making a hospital a desirable workplace.

nursing organizations were the first professional organizations for women in America. They were also the first professional organizations to be integrated—black nurses were accepted as full members. Nurses became a powerful force in the early women's movement.

Margaret Sanger (1879–1966), for example, was a public health nurse in New York City. After seeing the suffering among poor women caused by repeated childbearing and unsafe abortions, she became an activist for birth control. In 1916, Sanger opened a family planning clinic in Brooklyn, the first ever in the United States. It was raided by the police nine days later and Sanger was jailed for 30 days. It was only in 1924, with the help of wealthy patrons, that Sanger was finally able to open a legal birth control clinic. Sanger founded the American Birth Control League, which eventually became Planned Parenthood. Her pioneering efforts to provide safe, effective birth control was a major force in giving women control over their bodies and reproduction and empowering them to be independent, autonomous individuals. Sanger died in 1966, just a few months after the groundbreaking court decision in *Griswold v. Connecticut,* which finally legalized birth control for married couples.

Lillian Wald (1867–1940) became a nurse in 1891 with the goal of providing better health care for the residents of the teeming Lower East Side in New York City. Her work led to the foundation in 1895 of the Henry Street Settlement, a community center that provided health care, education, and many other services to the poor immigrants of the area. Lillian Wald championed the rights of women and children. Her work led to creation of the U.S. Children's Bureau in 1912 and strict limits on child labor. Lillian Wald is best remembered, however, for the creation of the visiting nurse service. She coined the term "public health nurse" in 1893 to describe nurses who visited the poor outside of hospitals, providing preventive care and teaching people about hygiene, good nutrition, and how to care for sick family members. By 1912, visiting nurses were recognized for their importance, and Wald and her colleagues in the public health movement recognized the need for the establishment of professional standards. They founded the National Organization of Public Health Nurses (NOPHN) to set professional standards and share ideas. Wald was elected as the organization's first president. Visiting nurses are still an important part of health care—in fact, a growing part as home health care even for serious illnesses becomes more common today.

At the start of the 19th century in America, most doctors practiced what they called "heroic medicine." Following the Hippocratic idea that the fluids of the body needed to balanced, they bled their patients, gave them powerful enemas and laxatives, raised blisters on their skin, and gave them purges to cause vomiting. They probably harmed or even killed far more patients than they helped. Not surprisingly, many people avoided doctors and chose traditional herbal treatments or simply hoped they would get better. The lack of effective medical treatment during this time meant that all sorts of quacks—people claiming to cure illness through unproven, unscientific methods—filled the void. Water treatments, restrictive diets, herbal treatments, electric shocks, hypnosis, patent medicines containing alcohol and opium, and many other useless ideas were popular, mostly for lack of other ideas. As the century progressed, however, the practice of medicine began to catch up to the new scientific ideas and tools, such as anesthesia using ether (first demonstrated in 1846) and the X-ray (discovered in 1896). In the United States, the idea of antiseptic surgery did not take hold until Dr. William Mayo began using the technique at his clinic in Minnesota in the late 1880s. His remarkable success and the other advances of the time showed that heroic medicine, herbalism, and quack remedies were no match for scientific medicine.

In response to the many worthless and even dangerous patent medicines that were in wide use during this time, the Food and Drugs Act of 1906 was signed into law by President Theodore Roosevelt. The law laid the foundation for the federal Food and Drug Administration (FDA), the agency that today oversees the safety of most food products, human and animal drugs, medical devices, and much more. The Food and Drugs Act was followed over the years by additional laws designed to improve the safety of drugs. In 1938, in response to a tainted medication that killed 107 people, the Federal Food, Drug, and Cosmetic Act was passed and signed into law by President Franklin D. Roosevelt. The new law greatly expanded the control and power of the Food and Drug Administration. It specifically gave the FDA the power to regulate drugs and make drug manufacturers prove that their drugs are safe before they can go on the market.

In the 1920s, vaccines against deadly diseases such as diphtheria, tetanus, and whooping cough were developed. Although other infectious diseases such as tuberculosis continued to be a serious problem, improved public health and sanitation helped to slow their growth. Hospitals continued to grow in size and in the services they offered, and nursing continued to grow as a profession. Specialized hospitals begin to appear—the first U.S. cancer hospital was dedicated in New York City in 1923.

Professionalizing Health Care

Throughout the 19th century, the quality of most medical education was very low. Pretty much anyone could start a medical school and pretty much anyone willing to pay the tuition could attend. The training was minimal—often only a few months—and many graduates never saw a patient or dissected a cadaver during their so-called training. They could call themselves medical doctors, but they had very little practical knowledge or clinical skills. Serious students who wanted to learn the new principles of scientific medicine often traveled to Germany or England to study.

Because there was no system of medical licensing, anyone with a medical degree, no matter how vaguely defined, could practice as a doctor. The situation began to improve in the 1860s. In 1869, Harvard extended the medical school year from four months to nine and began to require that students pass written exams. In 1876, Johns Hopkins University opened and introduced a much more rigorous curriculum, including extensive clinical practice. The American Hospital Association was founded in 1899 to set standards for hospital care. In 1910, Abraham Flexner conducted a groundbreaking study of medical schools for the American Medical Association. The report set new high standards for medical schools that effectively put most of the old-fashioned schools out of business.

Fast Facts

Medical Ingenuity

Earle Dickson's wife kept cutting her fingers in the kitchen. In 1921, Dickson, an employee of the medical supply company Johnson & Johnson, came up with an easy solution to his wife's constant need for small bandages: a one-piece bandage that combined surgical tape and gauze. His invention was christened the Band-Aid; Dickson went on to become a vice president of the company.

Just as medical schools became more scientific and professional starting in the late 1800s, nursing education was also becoming more serious. The influence of Florence Nightingale was felt strongly in America, as shown by the life of one of the most important nurses of the time, Linda Richards.

The first trained nurse to graduate from America's first school of nursing, Linda Richards (1841–1930) received her diploma from the New England Hospital for Women and Children in Boston in 1873. (The first African-American woman to earn her nursing diploma was Mary Eliza Mahoney, who graduated from the same pioneering program in 1879.) After her graduation, Richards moved to New York City and became a night supervisor at Bellevue Hospital. While there, she created a system of charts, or individual records for each patient, that was widely adopted in the United States and in England. Richards returned to Boston in 1874 and became superintendent of the Boston Training School for Nurses. She formed the program into one of the best in the country, but she was still dissatisfied with her results. To improve her own skills, she went to England in 1877 and studied at the Nightingale School. Florence Nightingale herself mentored Richards and encouraged her to return to America and work to improve nursing education. In 1885, she helped to establish the first nursing school in Japan, remaining there for five years. On her return to America, Richards was elected the first president of the American Society of Superintendents of Training Schools for Nurses. Like her mentor Florence Nightingale, Linda Richards worked tirelessly—and very effectively—to make nursing a respected profession based on solid training.

The American Society of Superintendents of Training Schools for Nurses was formed in 1893. It was the first organization for nursing in the United States and also the first professional organization of any kind for women. In 1912 the society was renamed the National League for Nursing Education (NLNE). In 1917, the NLNE released its first standard curriculum for schools of nursing. In 1952, the organization became the National League for Nursing (NLN), the name it goes by today. The organization took and still has the responsibility for accrediting nursing education programs across the country.

The many nursing schools that followed were usually associated with a hospital, although today most nursing schools are based at community colleges or traditional colleges and universities. The University of Minnesota was the first university-based nursing program, founded in 1909. The Yale School of Nursing in 1923 was the first to be entirely independent, with its own dean and faculty. In 1956, the Columbia University School of Nursing began offering a master's degree in nursing.

The true professionalization of nursing as a career happened in 1903, with the passage in New York State of the Nurse Practice Act, also known as the Armstrong Bill. This law set standards for nursing degrees and nursing practice and began the idea of the registered nurse as someone who has met a high standard of training and skills. Before the bill was passed, there were some 15,000 untrained nurses in New York and only about 2,500 nurses with formal training. Some of those with formal training had spent only a few months in a hospital setting, while others had trained for three years. After the law was passed, even many of the trained nurses could not meet the registration requirements because their nursing schools had provided only minimal training. The first nursing license in America was issued in 1904 to Ida Jane Anderson of Rochester.

By the time America entered World War I, nursing was an established profession. The nurses who served overseas during the conflict provided a level of care that had never been seen before in wartime. Wounded soldiers had a far better chance of survival than at any time in history. The aftermath of World War I led to the beginnings of physical therapy as a health care profession. The many soldiers with amputations needed help to regain as much function as possible and learn to use the new artificial limbs that were being developed. Hundreds of women were trained in crash courses to be "reconstruction aides," an early term for physical therapist. In 1921, the American Women's Physical Therapeutic Association was formed, with 274 charter members. It was the first professional association for physical therapists in the United States. By the end of the 1930s, the American Women's Physical Therapeutic Association had decided to admit men and changed its name to the American Physiotherapy Association; membership grew to about 1,000.

By the start of the 1920s, X-rays had became a standard tool for doctors and the profession of X-ray technician was beginning to be recognized. In 1920, a group of 13 X-ray technicians in Chicago formed the American Association of Radiological Technicians (now the American Association of Radiologic Technologists). These technicians had all been trained on the job but recognized the need for standardized classroom and clinical training. The first formal programs did not begin until 1933, however. Today, there are more than a thousand recognized programs for radiologic technologists.

Emergency medicine took a leap upward in 1929, when the first air ambulance began in New York City. This was the start of emergency air transport, which today uses helicopters to transport emergency patients to the level one trauma centers (those which are equipped to provide the highest level of surgical care to trauma patients), greatly improving the odds of survival for patients with serious injuries and burns.

The 1930s saw a very significant development, though it did not seem that way at the time: the founding of the National Institutes of Health in 1930. The first institute was the former Hygienic Laboratory at the Marine Hospital on Staten Island in New York, which dated back to 1887. In 1930, the Ransdell Act changed the name of the Hygienic Laboratory to National Institute (singular) of Health (NIH) and authorized the establishment of fellowships for research into basic biological and medical problems. Basic research remains the primary mission of the NIH to this day. In 1937, the second institute, the National Cancer Institute, was created, and the NIH became plural: the National Institutes of Health. In 1935, 92 acres of land near Bethesda, Maryland, were donated to the NIH. After World War II, the NIH grew rapidly and added additional institutes, such as the National Institute of Arthritis and Metabolic Diseases and the National Heart, Lung, and Blood Institute. By 1998, the NIH had 27 different institutes and centers. It is also the home of the National Library of Medicine (NLM), the world's largest medical library with a collection of more than 5.1 million items. The NLM manages Medline, a Web-based database that makes most current medical literature available to anyone at no cost. The work of the NIH over the decades has been extremely important. More than a hundred Nobel Prizes have been awarded based on NIH-supported research. Today the NIH invests more than $28 billion a year in medical research.

World War II saw huge changes in American medicine. Thousands of doctors and nurses served during the war, often in field hospitals near the front lines. More than 59,000 American nurses served in the Army Nurse Corps during World War II; more than 200 died in battle conditions. The American Red Cross played an important role in recruiting and training military nurses, using the slogan "American nurses for American men." Another health care specialty, nurse anesthetist, was born during this time. The Army developed a special six-month training program that taught more than 2,000 nurses how to administer inhalation anesthesia, blood and blood derivatives, and oxygen therapy as well as how to recognize, prevent, and treat shock. The military nurses who returned to civilian life brought with them huge amounts of experience that raised nursing to a higher level of responsibility and authority.

During the war, technological advances, such as the use of transfused blood, saved many lives. By 1943, penicillin was in widespread use on the battlefield. Considered a miracle drug for good reason, penicillin prevented and treated the infections that so often followed battlefield wounds. Many thousands of lives were saved—and the new age of modern antibiotics began.

Modern Health Care Begins

When the war was finally over, money poured into civilian health care. The network of Veteran's Administration hospitals was greatly expanded. In 1946, the Hill-Burton Act provided billions of dollars for a major expansion of hospitals and other health facilities over the next thirty years. The Act was designed to help reduce disparities in health care by providing more money for poorer states to improve existing hospitals and build new ones. Facilities that took the money had to make their services available to everyone living in the service area, regardless of race, color, or national origin. Big cracks in segregated health care began to appear.

During the war and during the nationwide polio epidemics of the 1940s and 1950s, physical therapists were in greater demand than ever before. Intensive training programs during World War II led to a large number of skilled therapists. By the late 1940s, the American Physiotherapy Association had become the American Physical Therapy Association (APTA), with more than 8,000 members. Physical therapy education programs had grown from 16 before the war to 39 by the late 1940s. By the 1960s, there were nearly 15,000 APTA members and 52 training programs. Today, APTA represents nearly 75,000 members in the United States, and there are 180 physical therapy education programs. In 1967, the physical therapist assistant category was created so that physical therapists could delegate some tasks and spend more time with patients. Today 236 institutions offer physical therapist assistant education programs.

Occupational therapy had been recognized as a profession ever since the early 1900s—the first recognized training program was established in 1906 in Boston. The field grew enormously during and following World War I. The National Society for the Promotion of Occupational Therapy was founded in 1917; the name was changed to the American Occupational Therapy Association (AOTA) in 1920, the name it still bears today. In 1923, the federal Industrial Rehabilitation Act gave OTs a big boost by mandating that any hospital treating victims of an industrial accident had to provide occupational therapy. In response, AOTA set up minimum standards for training programs. At the time, the program was 12 months long; students had to be high school graduates.

During World War II, every available trained therapist was called on to help treat injured soldiers and help them return to civilian life with as much independence as possible. They worked with soldiers who suffered from shell shock—what today is called post-traumatic stress disorder—and with those who had suffered physical injuries. Even so, it was not until 1947, when the war was over, that OTs were recognized as a military specialty. This recognition helped the profession expand in civilian life. In 1956, AOTA created the certified occupational therapy assistant title, allowing workers to join the field without the extensive training needed to be a full OT. When Medicare and Medicaid were created in 1965, occupational therapy was one of the services covered, and demand for these skilled professional rose. Demand rose again in 1975, when the important Education of the Handicapped Act was passed. Occupational therapy was covered as an essential service to help children gain skills and independence—and demand rose again. The Americans with Disabilities Act of 1990 and follow-on laws since then have made the work of occupational therapists and assistants even more important.

Fast Facts

How Do New Health Care Jobs Start?

The first blood bank in America was opened in 1937 at Chicago's Cook County Hospital. The blood bank used refrigeration to preserve blood products and followed strict equipment sterilization protocols. The number of patients who had bad reactions to transfusions dropped dramatically—and laboratory technician became a new job title.

In 1946, a group of "oxygen orderlies," doctors, nurses, and others met at the University of Chicago to form the Inhalational Therapy

Association. This was the first step toward creating the profession of respiratory therapist (RT). At first, because oxygen and other gases were contained in large, very heavy high-pressure cylinders, oxygen orderlies (sometimes jokingly called "gas jockeys") had to be strong young men. Later, as technological innovations such as oxygen concentrators made the heavy cylinders a thing of the past, respiratory therapy opened up to women. In the early days, most RTs had simply received informal on-the-job training. One of the first functions of the new association was to promote higher standards in treatment methods and to advance the knowledge of inhalation therapy through lectures and other means. In 1950, the New York Academy of Medicine published a report on standards for inhalation therapy that became the basis for formal education programs. Although the standards were widely praised, it was not until 1957 that they were put into practice; the first registration exam was not given until 1960. In 1982, the state of California passed the first licensing law for respiratory therapists. Other states followed, and in 2004 Vermont became the 48th state to pass a licensure law governing respiratory therapists. Respiratory therapists today are an integral part of the medical team, especially for patients in intensive care. In addition, because equipment such as respirators has become much smaller and less expensive, many people who cannot breathe on their own or who need extra oxygen can be treated at home instead of in the hospital; respiratory therapists are now an important part of the home health care system. Today the Inhalational Therapy Association has become the American Association for Respiratory Care (AARC), with more than 47,000 members nationwide.

Medical advances in the 1950s led to an increased demand for nurses—and to a serious nursing shortage. Part of the solution was to hand off some nursing responsibilities to new jobs in the growing area of allied health care. In 1952, President Truman's Commission on the Health Needs of the Nation issued a report that called for more paramedical workers. New job titles began to appear. Being an X-ray technician, for example, became a standard job title, while advances in nuclear medicine led to the new job title radiological technologist. The heart-lung machine, which allows for open-heart surgery, was invented in 1953. The first successful kidney transplant was performed in 1954; today more than 16,000 kidneys are transplanted every year in the United States. Surgical advances like this led to an increased need for critical care nurses to care for postoperative patients. Fortunately, the development of the first polio vaccine in 1952 by Jonas Salk led to mass immunization efforts and a significant drop in the number of polio cases.

Massive changes in health care came in the 1960s. The laws creating Medicaid and Medicare were enacted in 1965 and vastly expanded access to health care for the elderly and the poor. About 19 million people enrolled in Medicare within the first two months; expenditures in the first year of the program were about $2 billion. In 1972, Medicare was expanded to include people younger than 65 with long-term disabilities and to cover all patients with end-stage renal disease. This led to a major expansion of patients and to the rapid growth of kidney dialysis centers staffed by trained nurses and technicians. By making dialysis accessible and safe, many thousands of lives have been extended.

Today there are more than 43 million Medicare recipients, and expenditures exceed $340 billion a year. Medicaid and Medicare combined now account for about one-third of all health care spending.

Allied Health Care Takes Off

The increased demand for health care from greater access in the 1960s led to even more shortages of nurses and doctors—and even more incentive to expand jobs in allied health care. At the same time, the Hill-Burton Act of 1946 was expanded to build even more hospitals and to improve and modernize older hospitals. To help deal with shortages of medical personnel, the first nurse practitioner program in America was begun in 1965 at the University of Colorado. Other programs soon followed. In 1968, the Comprehensive Manpower Act was passed, designed to help increase the supply of primary care providers in the United States. The Act helps nurse practitioner programs expand even further. By 1973, there were more than 65 nurse practitioner training programs. By 1980, more than 200 nurse practitioner programs were available, and between 15,000 and 20,000 NPs were practicing. By 1997, every state recognized nurse practitioner as a formal title, and NPs had more authority to diagnose and prescribe for their patients. Today well more than 100,000 nurse practitioners work with patients, taking over many of the responsibilities of medical doctors.

In 1965, the National Academy of Science took a serious look at accidental deaths and injuries in the United States. They found that there were 52 million accidental injuries that killed 107,000 people, temporarily disabled more than 10 million, and permanently impaired 400,000 people—at a cost of $18 billion. The report concluded that the country needed a much better emergency response system. Congress responded by enacting the National Highway Safety Act of 1966. The Act provided millions in federal funding to create a national standard curriculum for emergency medical technicians (EMTS) and paramedics. The law said that states receiving federal highway construction funds would lose 10 percent of the amount unless they established emergency services. Needless to say, the states complied. This led to the formal creation of EMT as a job title with a defined course of study. In 1970, the National Registry of EMTs was created to set a national standard for education, exams, and certification.

In 1967, Congress passed the Allied Health Professions Personnel Training Act. This important law radically changed how allied health professionals were seen—it professionalized the jobs. The Act systematized and improved training in allied health care areas such as physical therapy, respiratory therapy, and licensed practical nursing. It raised the professional standards and mandated certification and licensing for many health care workers. It also set high standards for educational programs that train health care workers. In response to the law, in 1967 the deans of thirteen university-based schools of allied health professions formed the Association of Schools of Allied Health Professions (ASAHP). They were responding to an urgent need for the schools to work together to improve the quality of allied health education and to increase the number of students graduating from training programs. ASAHP played a leading role in setting a high standard and helping new schools of allied health open and meet their accreditation requirements. Today, the accreditation work for allied health schools has been largely taken over by the Commission on Accreditation of Allied Health Education Programs

Fast Facts

New Technology, New Jobs

In 1945, the first artificial kidney machine, made with laundry tubs and cellophane tubing, was in use. This machine is the forerunner of today's complex dialysis machines, used to keep patients with kidney failure alive. Another new job description—dialysis technician—came into being.

(CAAHEP), which now reviews and accredits more than two thousand educational programs in twenty health science occupations. The remarkable growth in high-quality training programs over the past decades goes directly back to the forward-looking Act of 1967.

The Allied Health Professions Personnel Training Act led directly to new programs to train physician assistants. The first surgeon's assistant program began at the University of Alabama in 1967; the first class of physician assistants (three men) graduated from Duke University that same year. By 1968, the first undergraduate program for PAs was established at Alderson-Broaddus College in Philippi, West Virginia. In 1969, a pioneering program trained ex-military corpsmen to be PAs capable of running rural primary care practices. This highly successful approach is still in use today in rural areas that are medically underserved. In 1973, the first certifying exam was given for PAs. By 1985, more than 10,000 PAs belonged to the American Association of Physician Assistants. As of 2000, when the state of Mississippi finally granted approval, PAs can practice in all fifty states. Today, more than 50,000 PAs are practicing in the United States. In addition to filling in for doctors in underserved areas across the country, PAs work as part of medical teams that provide care for complex medical problems.

The education of allied health professionals continued to be an issue. National standards for high-quality programs were lacking in many areas, and schools that wanted to set up training programs needed guidance. In 1978, the National Commission on Allied Health Education issued a report calling for the creation of overall standards for training programs to raise admission requirements and set minimum requirements for classroom and clinical work. This work turned out to be very challenging. Allied health care workers are a very diverse group, and it is difficult to come up with overall recommendations that apply to all of them. Even so, the basic ideas of minimum educational standards and national certification programs were soon accepted by schools and professional organizations, and allied health care took another big step forward.

The National Commission recommendations made professional organizations take a closer look at the job titles that were in use. This led to some upheaval and controversy. Since the 1940s, for instance, the American Dietetic Association had been offering training for a dietetic support position called food service supervisor. In the late 1950s, correspondence courses that could substitute for in-person training were added. In the late 1960s, the job title was changed to dietetic assistant, and in 1972 the ADA attempted to formalize the job definition and training requirements. Because dietetic assistants were performing many different functions, ranging from work that overlapped with that of a registered dietitian to clerical work that could easily have been done by a secretary, the organization's leaders could not come to agreement. It was not until 1983 that the job title dietetic technician registered was created—and that was done by a separate professional organization created under the ADA umbrella to represent dietetic techs.

Tightened Medicare and Medicaid requirements starting in late 1980s were another good reason for standardizing job descriptions and defining exactly what each worker could and could not do. Hospitals, nursing homes, and doctors who wanted to receive Medicare and Medicaid reimbursement had to meet strict quality standards, including having well-trained allied health workers who could meet national accreditation requirements. This meant that many skilled workers who had been trained on the job in areas such as laboratory technology and respiratory therapy had to pass certification exams. Jobs that did not have any formal training, such as being an aide in a nursing home, now had stricter requirements. The job title certified nursing assistant (CNA) came into existence.

As medical care became ever more complex, new allied health careers arose. Cardiovascular technology, for example, was recognized by the Commission on Accreditation of Allied Health Education Programs (CAAHEP) as an allied health profession in 1981. Diagnostic medical sonographer and other jobs, such as nuclear medicine technologist and radiation therapy technologist, also date back to the 1980s.

The 1990s to Today

The 1990s were a decade of important health care legislation with lasting impact. Two laws in particular had a major affect on health care workers. The first was the Americans with Disabilities Act, passed in 1990. This law created new demand for physical therapists, occupational therapists, and others to help Americans with disabilities live independent, dignified lives. The second was the Health Insurance Portability and Accountability Act of 1996, better known as HIPAA. This act, along with additional regulations in 2002, set rigorous new standards for patient privacy and record keeping. The law affects every health care worker and every patient every day.

Another important concept of the 1990s is the magnet hospital—a hospital so good that the best nurses are drawn to work there as if by magnets—and then are kept there by the magnetism. Magnet hospitals are designated by the American Nurses Credentialing Center. This highly desired designation was first awarded to the University of Washington Medical Center in Seattle in 1994. There are now more than 251 hospitals in 44 states that have been awarded this coveted distinction.

When Medicare was first enacted, it did not include a benefit to pay for prescription drugs. The reason was that in 1965, there simply were not that many drugs available to treat even common problems such as high blood pressure. Drugs to treat cancer were still a vision, and drugs for diseases such as heart failure were not very helpful. The lawmakers simply did not see the need to pay for the handful of drugs in use then. The explosion of medical knowledge and the many new life-saving drugs in the decades since meant that many Medicare recipients were being kept alive and well by drugs they could not afford. In 2003, new legislation added a drug benefit to Medicare, making it much less costly for recipients to buy their drugs. Demand for pharmacy techs began to rise, a trend that is expected to continue well into the future.

The basic concepts of the Americans with Disabilities Act of 1990 were expanded in 2004 with the Individuals with Disabilities Education Act (IDEA) of 2004. This law ensures services such as speech therapy, physical therapy, and occupational therapy for some 6.5 million eligible children, ranging from infants to youths with disabilities. IDEA has added to the already strong demand for therapists and assistants in these areas.

Patient safety in hospitals was improved in 2005, when the Patient Safety and Quality Improvement Act was passed. This law provides for the confidential reporting of medical errors to patient safety organizations. The law had the effect of making hospitals take patient safety and medical errors even more seriously than they already did. It led to a surprising amount of innovation in a short period. This has been especially important in helping to battle MRSA (methicillin-resistant *Staphylococcus aureus*). This extremely dangerous strain of staph infection was created by overuse of antibiotics. It is resistant to just about every available antibiotic and is becoming increasingly common, especially in hospitals. Hospitalized patients, already weakened due to their illness, are very susceptible to MRSA. Strict infection control by well-trained staff is the only way to combat MRSA.

Professional
Ethics

African-American Nurses in World War II

The Army Nurse Corps had very few African-American nurses during World War II. When the war ended in September 1945 just 479 black nurses were serving in a corps of 50,000. All the armed forces were segregated, and the Army argued that it did not need many black nurses because they were only allowed to care for black troops in black wards or hospitals. Although segregation was still very much in place in America, public outrage and political pressure forced the Army to drop its quota system in 1944.

The first black medical unit to deploy overseas was the 25th Station Hospital Unit, which contained thirty nurses. The unit went to Liberia in 1943 to care for U.S. troops protecting strategic airfields and rubber plantations. By the end of the war, black nurses had served in Africa, England, Burma, and the southwest Pacific. These courageous women never received the recognition they deserved, and they returned home to a society that had fought for freedom around the world but still denied it to many of its black citizens. Times have changed in the decades since then, but to this day African-Americans are still very under-represented in the health care professions. In addition, African-Americans often have less access to health care and often receive care that is not as good as it should be. Many concerned health care professionals are active in organizations and programs that help recruit more minorities into their fields. Ethical health care workers need to be aware of the disparities in their professions and in care and make every effort to provide quality health care to everyone.

Allied health care workers now make up about 60 percent of the United States health care workforce, or about seven million workers. More than two hundred professions fall into the allied health care category, and health care jobs are expected to be among the fastest-growing positions in the country over the coming years. They work mostly in nearly six thousand hospitals with more than a million beds and some five million employees and treat over 37 million inpatients each year. Allied health care workers also help treat about

118 million people in the hospital emergency room, help care for over 481 million outpatients in hospital clinics, and help deliver four million babies each year.

Health care workers today can look ahead to a future that will include expanded access to health care—and expanded demand for health care workers. Serious effort will be made to eliminate disparities and provide high-quality health care to every American. At the same time, health care costs are rising very rapidly, and there will be a lot of pressure to keep down expenses, including the cost of paying workers. Many of the battles over costs will take place over issues such as Medicare reimbursements, high drug prices, and the cost of the latest medical equipment. Going forward, most skilled health care workers can still expect to have secure jobs with good pay.

A Brief Chronology

Prehistory: Traditional healers use herbs and simple techniques to treat illnesses, injuries, and aid women in childbirth. Shamans use healing magic.

460 B.C.E.: Hippocrates of Cos, the first true physician, is born in ancient Greece. Hippocrates observes patients systematically, writes case histories, and lays the foundation of scientific medicine.

Second century C.E.: Galen, a Roman physician of Greek origin, moved medicine forward with studies of anatomy, systematic observations of patients, and new ideas in surgery.

1514–1564: Andreas Vesalius, the founder of modern anatomy, uses human dissection to discover, among other things, that the human heart has four chambers. Vesalius dares to show that Galen was often wrong.

1628: The English physician William Harvey publishes a book describing the circulation of the blood.

1751: The first American hospital, Pennsylvania General Hospital in Philadelphia, opens.

1821: Massachusetts General Hospital in Boston opens.

1846: Anesthesia using ether is demonstrated for the first time by dentist William Thomas Green Morton at the Massachusetts General Hospital.

1854: Florence Nightingale and her nurses arrive in the Crimea and begin to improve the military hospitals. The death rate for hospitalized British soldiers drops from 42 percent to under 3 percent.

1860: Florence Nightingale publishes her highly influential book *Notes on Nursing: What It Is and What It Is Not.* Today this work is considered a classic introduction to the art and science of nursing

1860s: Louis Pasteur in France formulates the germ theory of infection, develops the pasteurization process to kill bacteria in liquids such as milk, and develops the concept of vaccination for diseases such as anthrax, rabies, and cholera.

1867: Joseph Lister discovers the use of carbolic acid as an antiseptic in surgery. Infection rates drop dramatically.

1873: Linda Richards becomes the first trained nurse to graduate from the New England Hospital for Women and Children in Boston, America's first school of nursing.

1876: Johns Hopkins University opens and introduces a rigorous medical curriculum, including extensive clinical practice.

1880s: The germ theory and the concept of antiseptic surgery gain widespread acceptance in the United States.

1881: Clara Barton, renowned for her work in organizing Union hospitals during the Civil War, founds the American Red Cross.

1890: Robert Koch of Germany publishes his four postulates, rules that are used to establish a causal relationship between a particular microbe and a disease.

1893: Lillian Wald (1867–1940) creates the visiting nurse service and coins the phrase "public health nurse." The American Society of Superintendents of Training Schools for Nurses is formed; it is the first organization for nursing in the United States and also the first professional organization of any kind for women.

1895: X-rays are discovered by Wilhelm Roentgen in Germany.

1899: The American Hospital Association is founded to set high standards for hospital care.

1903: The New York State Nurse Practice Act, also known as the Armstrong Bill, professionalizes nursing and creates the registered nurse concept.

1904: The first nursing license in America is issued to Ida Jane Anderson of Rochester, New York.

1906: The Food and Drugs Act of 1906 is signed into law by President Theodore Roosevelt. The law lays the foundation for the federal Food and Drug Administration (FDA).

1909: The University of Minnesota founds the first university-based nursing program.

1910: Abraham Flexner conducts a groundbreaking study of medical schools for the American Medical Association. The Flexner report sets new high standards for medical schools.

1916: Margaret Sanger opens a family planning clinic in Brooklyn, the first ever in the United States. It was almost immediately closed by authorities; not until 1924 was Sanger able to open a legal clinic.

1921: The Band-Aid is invented.

1923: The Yale School of Nursing opens and is the first to be entirely independent, with its own dean and faculty.

1930: The first laboratory of what would become the National Institutes of Health is founded.

1937: The first blood bank in America opens at Chicago's Cook County Hospital.

1938: The Federal Food, Drug, and Cosmetic Act is signed into law by President Franklin D. Roosevelt. The new law greatly expands the control and power of the Food and Drug Administration.

1939–1945: More than 59,000 American nurses serve in the Army Nurse Corps during World War II; more than 200 die in battle conditions. Penicillin is introduced and saves thousands of soldiers.

1945: The first artificial kidney machine, made with laundry tubs and cellophane tubing, is in use—the forerunner of today's complex dialysis machines.

1946: The Hill-Burton Act provides billions of dollars for a major expansion of hospitals and other health facilities across the country over the next thirty years.

1952: President Truman's Commission on the Health Needs of the Nation issues a report that calls for more paramedic and allied health care workers. Jonas Salk develops the first polio vaccine.

1953: The heart-lung machine, which allows for open-heart surgery, is invented.

1954: The first successful kidney transplant is performed.

1956: The Columbia University School of Nursing begins offering a master's degree in nursing.

1965: Medicare and Medicaid are created, bringing health care to millions of poor and elderly Americans. The first nurse practitioner program in America begins at the University of Colorado.

1966: The National Highway Safety Act provides federal funding to create a national standard curriculum for emergency medical technicians (EMTs) and paramedics.

1967: The Allied Health Professions Personnel Training Act improves training, raises professional standards, and mandates certification and licensing for many health care workers. The first class of physician assistants (three men) graduate from Duke University.

1968: The Comprehensive Manpower Act increases the number of allied health programs and practitioners.

1972: The first CAT scan machine in America is installed at the Mayo Clinic.

1975: The Education of the Handicapped Act creates new demand for occupational therapists, physical therapists, and other professionals.

1980: The World Health Organization announces that smallpox has been eradicated.

1983: HIV, the virus that causes AIDS, is identified.

1990: The Americans with Disabilities Act creates even more demand for therapists.

1994: The first magnet hospital designation is awarded to the University of Washington Medical Center in Seattle.

1996: The Health Insurance Portability and Accountability Act, known as HIPAA, sets rigorous new standards for patient privacy and record keeping.

2003: New legislation adds a drug benefit to Medicare, making it much less costly for recipients to buy their drugs.

2004: The Americans with Disabilities Act of 1990 is expanded by the Individuals with Disabilities Education Act (IDEA).

2005: Patient safety in hospitals is by the Patient Safety and Quality Improvement Act. The law provides for the confidential reporting of medical errors to patient safety organizations.

Chapter 2

State of the Industry

Health care is the largest industry in the United States—in 2009, health care provided more than 14 million jobs at every level. Jobs in the industry range from highly paid physicians and hospital executives to hourly workers such as home health care aides. In between are hundreds of job titles offering steady employment and good salaries or hourly pay. In fact, according to the Bureau of Labor Statistics, average earnings for workers in most areas of health care are higher than they are for workers in any other private industry.

Never has every aspect of the health care industry been in greater need of enthusiastic new workers. At every job level, today and for the next ten years or more, there is a very serious shortage of health care workers. Right now, for example, the shortage of nurses is so severe that one in every 10 nursing jobs is open.

Some of the fastest growing occupations in the nation are related to health care, including home health aides, pharmacy technicians, and physical therapy assistants. In 2008, health care had a net gain of 419,000 jobs. Health care will generate three million new jobs between now and 2016, more than any other industry. The new jobs will be in every area of health care at every level of training. Opportunities to enter the field and move ahead have never been greater.

Where Are the Jobs?

Health care workers are generally employed in hospitals, nursing and residential care facilities, practitioners' offices, home health care services, outpatient care facilities and in a variety of other settings.

What follows is a closer look at where your health care career could start or take you.

Hospitals

Although hospitals make up only about 1 percent of all health care establishments, they employ 35 percent of all workers. In 2008, total employment in the nation's hospitals reached nearly five million people—most of them health care providers of various sorts. Employment in hospitals will continue to grow. According to the Bureau of Labor Statistics, hospital employment will increase by 13 percent between 2006 and 2016.

Nationwide, there are over 11,000 hospitals. In 2008, 7,878 of the country's hospitals, or about 72 percent, were privately owned community hospitals. Most are owned and operated by a nonprofit organization. For-profit hospitals are a smaller part of the industry, with less than a thousand hospitals. State and local governments operate over 2,400 hospitals, and the federal government operates 286, mostly as part of the Veterans Administration. Although the current trend is to close or merge small or underused hospitals, the aging American population—combined with greater health care access— means increasing demand for hospital services in the future. Many larger hospitals will expand their facilities, adding more patient beds and also more outpatient services such as cancer care centers. Larger hospitals mean more high-paying jobs at every level.

Hospitals provide complete medical care, ranging from emergency room services to diagnostic services to surgery and continuous nursing care. The care a hospital provides may be on an inpatient basis, where the patient stays in the hospital at least overnight, or on an outpatient basis, where treatment such as physical therapy is provided at the hospital and the patient then leaves. A small community hospital offers primary care that can handle most emergencies and common health issues, such as a heart attack or having a baby. Larger regional hospitals, also called secondary hospitals, usually offer all medical services in most specialties. Tertiary hospitals are highly specialized, focusing on a particular health problem such as cancer or on a particular population, such as children. More than 70 percent of all jobs in hospitals are in large hospitals that employ more than a thousand workers. Roughly three out of 10 hospital workers are registered nurses; about one in five hospital jobs are in service occupations such as nursing and patient aides. Hospitals also employ large numbers of office and administrative staff workers, such as medical secretaries and medical billers—people who are essential for keeping the hospital running smoothly but who have little or no contact with patients.

Average earnings for hospital workers are higher than for the overall health care industry. This is because many hospital jobs, such as registered nurse or X-ray technician, require a high level of education and training. The skilled staff members at a tertiary hospital are among the most highly paid workers in all of health care.

Nursing and Residential Care Facilities

Overall, nursing homes and residential care facilities make up about 11.5 percent of all health care establishments, but they employ 23 percent of all health care workers, or about 2,901,000 people in 2006. Of these, about two out of three are in service occupations such as nursing and certified nursing assistants. The Bureau of Labor Statistics projects that employment in this area will be up 23.7 percent between 2006 and 2016.

Nationwide, there are about 16,100 Medicare-approved nursing homes, also called skilled nursing facilities. They serve about 1.5 million residents, most of them over age 65. Nursing homes provide inpatient nursing, rehabilitation, and health-related personal care to people who need round-the-clock health care. Residents in nursing homes need long-term care and cannot live independently, but they do not need to be in a hospital. In the nursing home, residents get the skilled nursing care they need, along with medical services and therapies.

Registered nurses supervise the care in these facilities, but almost all the direct patient care is done by licensed practical or vocational nurses or by certified nursing assistants. Therapists such as occupational therapists or speech-language pathologists also work in nursing homes; so do dietitians and nutritionists. The administrative staff of a nursing home or residential care facility is small, especially when compared to a hospital.

As the population ages—80 million baby boomers will reach the age of 65 starting in 2010—the demand for beds in these facilities will increase, and so will the demand for workers at every level. The number of certified nursing homes in the United States has actually been dropping steadily. In 1985, there were over 19,000 homes, but many were small and could not meet the tough new Medicare standards that were enacted in 1987. While smaller facilities have

Everyone
Knows

How to Lose Your License

Doctors, registered nurses, licensed practical or vocational nurses, dietitians, physical therapists, and many other health care professional are licensed by states where they work. Losing your license means you cannot legally work in your professional area. States are usually reluctant to revoke licenses, but there are some things that will put your license in danger or cause it to be pulled, including:

- Being covicted of a felony such as theft, insurance fraud, drunk driving, assault, or drug possession
- Being addicted to drugs or alcohol
- Failing a drug test
- Abusing patients physically or verbally
- Making a life-threatening error, such as giving the wrong medication
- Failing to meet continuing education requirements
- Failing to renew your license on a timely basis

As a general rule, someone whose license is in danger can appeal to the relevant state authorities to keep it or have it restored. Someone with a drug problem, for instance, can agree to complete a treatment program as an alternative to license revocation, and might agree to restrictions on where he or she can work in the future. Most states are very willing to give health care workers a second chance as long as patient care and safety are not endangered.

closed, larger facilities have grown, adding beds and providing more services. This trend is very likely to continue. As with hospitals, larger nursing homes generally offer higher pay, more types of jobs, and more opportunity for advancement. In addition, many hospitals have expanded into long-term care services and are operating nursing homes and other facilities as part of the larger system.

Working in a nursing home is challenging but also very rewarding. About 75 percent of all nursing home residents over age 65 need help with activities of daily living such as dressing, eating, and bathing. Sadly, about 42 percent of all residents have Alzheimer's disease or dementia, and about 12 percent have other psychiatric conditions such as mood disorders. These patients deserve compassionate treatment from caring workers, even when they cannot remember who you are. That is not always easy—it takes patience, a positive attitude, and a sense of humor. The work in a nursing home can also be physically demanding, because residents often need help with moving around—from their bed to a chair, for instance. On-the-job injuries and illnesses are higher than average for nursing home workers. The national average for private industry is 4.4 injuries or illnesses per hundred workers, but for nursing home employees, the rate goes up to 9.8. Health care workers involved with direct patient care need to be extra-careful to avoid back strain from lifting patients; they also need to be careful about handling contaminated materials such as needles and bandages.

Residential care facilities are designed for residents who need less medical attention but still need round-the-clock help and supervision. Many residents need at least some help with all the usual activities of daily living, such as getting dressed, bathing, eating, and moving around, while others can live more independently. Examples of residential care facilities include rehabilitation centers (also known as convalescent homes), assisted living residences, group homes, and alcohol and drug rehabilitation centers. The care at these facilities is not always supervised by a registered nurse because the residents may not really need much nursing care. In a group home for developmentally disabled adults, for instance, the residents primarily need supervision and some help with activities of daily living, but do not usually need much medical assistance. The staff members at these facilities are mostly certified nursing assistants or home health care aides. Larger facilities often have staff therapists such as occupational therapists, but smaller facilities usually hire therapists on a contract basis or send residents to outpatient facilities.

Doctors' Offices

About 37 percent of all health care establishments are the offices of physicians in private practice. These offices employ about 17 percent of all workers; in 2006, that meant about 2,154,000 people. Employment prospects in this area are good—the Bureau of Labor Statistics says that employment will grow by nearly 25 percent between 2006 and 2016.

In addition to the professional staff and registered nurses, doctors' offices employ a lot of office and administrative support workers such as medical coders and billers. Doctors' offices can range from a single practitioner with a small staff to large group practices or clinics with many physicians and a large number of staff members. Most offices are fairly small, however. Over 85 percent of non-hospital health care establishments employ fewer than 20 workers. Nearly half have only one to four employees; nearly 40 percent have five to 19 employees. Only about 3 percent employ a hundred or more workers—but those practices employ 39 percent of the workers in the area.

Because many doctors' offices are fairly small, most workers will have a lot of contact with patients before, during, and after the time they spend with the doctor or nurse. The pace can sometimes be hectic—the telephone rings constantly and a steady stream of patients passes through the office every day. In addition, in a small office, one worker may have a lot of different responsibilities or may be asked to cover for another worker. Flexibility and being able to work under pressure are good attributes.

Dentists' Offices

Dentists' offices are a surprisingly large area for health care, making up about 20 percent, or one in five, of all health care establishments. They employ 6.3 percent of all health care workers, almost all of them dental hygienists. Nationwide, there are 163,000 dental hygienists. Most dental practices are small and employ only a few workers in addition to just one to five dentists. Many practices offer general dentistry services; others specialize in a particular area such as periodontics (gum problems) or orthodontics (braces and other treatments for crooked teeth).

The aging American population means that more and more people will have trouble with their teeth and gums over the next few decades. Not surprisingly, job growth for dental hygienists will be very high. The Bureau of Labor Statistics projects an increase in jobs of 30 percent between 2006 and 2016.

Home Health Care Services

This large and rapidly growing area employs about 7 percent of all health workers. In 2008, this area grew by 64,000 jobs. About

Everyone

Knows

Handling Sharps

A needle stick or cut from a scalpel can lead to infection with the hepatitis B virus or HIV, which causes AIDS. According to OSHA, every year about 8,700 health care workers get hepatitis B, and about 200 will die as a result. The best way to prevent sticks and cuts is to dispose of sharps—needles, scalpels, scissors, and other sharp objects—immediately after use. OSHA requires that puncture-resistant containers to dispose of sharps be available as near as possible to the area of use. The containers must be leakproof and have a lid. They are usually colored bright red or clearly labeled so that everyone knows the contents are hazardous. Never reach into the container!

582,000 people are home health aides, people who work directly with clients to help them with the activities of daily living, such as getting dressed and eating, and with simple medical needs. In addition, many other health care professionals also provide home-based services to clients. Nurses, physical therapists, and many others visit clients in their homes and provide treatment such as intravenous drug infusion. According to Medicare statistics, the number of beneficiaries using home health services grew by 17 percent between 2002 and 2006. Today more than 2.8 million people are receiving home health care just through the Medicare program. Many more are getting the services through other means, including by paying for it themselves.

Today many patients who once would have needed hospital or nursing home care can remain in their own homes with the help of home health care services. Most are elderly, but today many disabled people also receive home health care services that let them lead independent lives. Treating people at home whenever possible is not just more convenient and less disruptive for them—it saves a lot of money. That is one big reason why home health care services is the single fastest growing area of the entire health care industry today. Another is the aging population. As more and more baby boomers reach age 65 and beyond, the need for home health care will only grow. The Bureau of Labor Statistics projects employment growth for home health aides at a whopping 46.9 percent between 2006 and 2016, more than any other area of health care. Much of the employment is with agencies, both nonprofit and profit-making, that send workers to the homes of clients. Other sources of employment are hospital-based home-care programs and working directly for clients.

Being a home health aide is not always easy. The work can be physically demanding, the hours can be long, sometimes night and weekend work is required, and the pay is on the low end for health care workers. Why do so many people want to do this work? Because being a home health aide is a great way to enter the health care field. It is a good starting point for continuing your education and moving up to more skilled positions such as licensed practical nurse or certified nursing assistant. These skills are also in demand in the home health area—and they can also lead to good jobs in hospitals and nursing homes.

Other Health Practitioners

This catchall term includes practitioners such as dietitians, audiologists, and physical therapists, along with practitioners of alternative medicine such as acupuncturists and naturopaths. These practitioners provide services directly to patients at their offices and usually have small staffs. Roughly two out of five jobs in this area are for professionals, but these offices also employ many office and support workers, including assistants, techs, medical billers, and medical secretaries—in all, about 571,000 people work in this area. The job outlook is good. The Bureau of Labor Statistics predicts that jobs in this area will grow by 28 percent between 2006 and 2016.

Outpatient Care Centers

A wide variety of specialized facilities care for patients who come on an outpatient basis for treatment. Examples include kidney dialysis centers, radiation centers, medical clinics, ambulatory surgery centers, urgent-care centers, and outpatient substance abuse clinics. Some outpatient care centers can be quite large, with many doctors and large staffs. As hospitals continue to consolidate and get bigger, more and more are building outpatient care centers—this will continue to be a growth area for some time to come. This part of the health care industry employs many highly trained workers, such as registered nurses, radiological technologists, and physical therapists. About 489,000 people, including many administrative workers, are employed in this area. Job growth is predicted to be 24 percent between 2006 and 2016.

Other Ambulatory Health Care Services
The "other" category of ambulatory health care services is a fairly small and specialized segment of the health care industry. It includes highly specialized services such as medical helicopter transport services, ambulance services, blood and organ banks, and monitoring services for people with pacemakers and other medical devices. Because this area includes ambulance services, it employs about two out of every five emergency medical technicians and paramedics. Overall, about 216,000 people are employed in this area. Growth here will be robust, according to the Bureau of Labor Statistics. Between 2006 and 2016, jobs will increase by 32 percent.

Medical and Diagnostic Laboratories
Medical and diagnostic labs provide services such as blood analysis and tests such as X-rays and CT scans, and perform other clinical tests such as diagnostic ultrasonography. Some labs are part of hospitals or outpatient care centers, while others are stand-alone centers. This is the smallest area of the health care industry in terms of total number of jobs, with about 202,000 employees. Growth here is lower than in other areas of health care—jobs are predicted to increase by only 17 percent between 2006 and 2016. Most lab workers such as diagnostic ultrasonographers are highly trained, however, and are in demand across the whole range of health care employers. Lab technicians and radiologic technologists and technicians make up about 44 percent of all jobs in this part of the industry. Many administrative workers, such as medical assistants and transcriptionists, work in labs.

What Do Health Care Workers Do?

The health care field is very large and very varied, which means that health care workers do all sorts of jobs and can have many different skills and specialties. All those jobs are essential for delivering high-quality care and keeping hospitals, clinics, and other health centers running smoothly.

Only about 4 percent of all health care professionals are doctors. Almost all the rest are allied health care workers. Sixteen percent are nurses and 5 percent are licensed practical nurses. An additional 9.5 percent are nursing aides and attendants. Just over 30 percent of employees—about six million people—are allied health workers such as respiratory therapists and dietitians. In all, some 60 percent of the health care workforce is allied health personnel.

Who are the allied health workers? They are the many health care providers with formal education and clinical training in their specialty. Most allied health workers have formal credentials—they are required to be certified, registered, or licensed. The list of allied health care careers is long and includes areas such as physical therapy, medical lab technologist, dental hygienist, and emergency medical technicians. In fact, the American Medical Association lists over 80 different allied health care professions. The Health Professions Network, a voluntary national group representing over 75 educational and professional organizations, says there are over 200 allied health professions!

No matter how you count health care professions, there is no doubt that this is the fastest-growing employment area in the country. According to the Bureau of Labor Statistics, of the fastest-growing 30 occupations from all industries nationwide, nearly a third are in health care. Take at look at this table, which shows projections from 2006 to 2016:

Fastest-Growing Health Care Jobs		
Rank	Occupation	% Growth Expected
2	Personal and home care aides	51
3	Home health aides	49
8	Medical assistants	35
15	Physical therapy assistants	32
16	Pharmacy technicians	32
18	Dental hygienists	30
29	Physical therapists	27
30	Physician assistants	27

Source: Bureau of Labor Statistics

Overall, job opportunities in all health care employment settings are good. Today the health care industry is poised on the edge of changes that will almost certainly lead to tremendous growth in employment.

The Outlook for Health Care Workers

The number of people moving into older age groups, with much higher needs for health care, is large and is growing faster than the overall population. This is leading to higher employment in home health care and in nursing and residential care. Advances in medical technology mean that people who are very sick or severely injured have a better chance of survival—but will also need more treatment, such as physical therapy and other help, to recover. More technology also means more demand for skilled technicians who can operate complex machinery such as CT scanners. Most importantly, access to medical care will increase with health insurance

Fast
Facts

The Drug Business

Today about 10 cents of every health care dollar goes to prescription drugs (by comparison, about 31 cents goes to hospital care). That means billions each year for medicines—the drug business is big business. The United States is the world's biggest market for drugs—we use about 48 percent of the world total. Partly because of our inefficient health care system, we spend more than any other nation as well. Per capita expenditure on drugs in 2006 was $1,069, nearly twice the amount in the rest of the world. An aging and unhealthy population, along with research breakthroughs for drugs that treat serious diseases such as cancer, mean that the pharmaceutical industry is growing almost as fast as the health care industry. The Bureau of Labor Statistics says about 292,000 people work in the pharmaceutical business and medicine manufacturing. Employment in the area is expected to rise by about 23 percent between 2006 and 2016.

reforms. Many Americans that once could not afford medical treatment will now be able to obtain it. It is too early to say exactly how this will impact health care workers, but an increase in patients will create an increase in the need for workers. One estimate from U.S. Department of Health and Human Services Bureau of Health Professions says that with universal health insurance the nation will need nearly 1.1 million doctors by 2020: that is 300,000 more doctors than we have now. Clearly, the impact will be felt in every aspect of health care. Demand for allied health care workers—especially those who assist doctors, such as nurse practitioners—is likely to go up the fastest.

Perhaps the largest growth area will be in the workforce outside the hospital setting. Hospital care is very expensive. To help control costs, patients are increasingly treated at outpatient facilities or at home. Workers will need to look beyond hospitals for employment to outpatient clinics and other alternative care sites. But because the health care workforce today has many older workers, many will retire over the coming years, opening up many positions across all health care settings. At the same time, immigration restrictions are slowing the number of foreign health care workers entering the United States, again opening positions in every setting.

In other areas, the aging population will also need more dental care, increasing the demand for dental hygienists. In the management area, skilled workers in information technology and electronic medical records are likely to be in very high demand. Rapid growth is also expected for jobs in management, business, and financial operations, even as hospitals and other establishments try to streamline management to save on administrative costs.

A career in health care does not always require a college education or an advanced degree. You can start a career as a registered nurse with a two-year associate's degree from a community college program, for example. You can enter other career paths, such as becoming an EMT, medical assistant, certified nursing assistant (CNA), or physical therapy assistant, with much shorter training courses. Everyone in health care, at every level, is always encouraged to learn additional skills that make you a better caregiver and can also help you move up the career ladder. A CNA or EMT, for instance, could take part-time classes to become a licensed practical or vocational nurse—and from there could continue taking courses that will lead to nursing degree. For motivated workers who are willing to spend the extra time on education, health care offers many excellent opportunities for moving up to better jobs, with more responsibility and higher pay.

A Closer Look at the Workplace

Hospitals are the largest employers of health care workers in the country. The Bureau of Labor Statistics reports that in 2009, the total number of all hospital employees was about 4.7 million. Of those, about half provide care directly to patients. Registered nurses are the largest group of health care workers in hospitals, with 1,485,130 employed in 2009. After that comes nursing aides, orderlies, and attendants, with 417,810 employed in 2009. There were 183,960 licensed practical nurses and licensed vocational nurses, 122,260 radiologic technologists and technicians, and 100,150 medical and clinical laboratory technologists.

How Much Do Health Care Workers Make?

Most health care workers make more money on average than most other workers in private industry. According to the Bureau of Labor Statistics, the average weekly earnings for a worker in private industry is $568; the average weekly earnings for a health care worker is $623. The difference also applies to the average hourly rate. In private industry, workers earn $16.76 an hour on average; health care workers have an average hourly wage of $18.73. Balancing this, however, is that hospital workers earn considerably more than average, while workers in nursing homes and home health care workers usually earn less than average. In health care as in other industries, the more training, skills, and experience you have, the more money you can make.

Earnings for health care workers also vary quite a bit depending on your occupation, which sector of the industry you work in, and whether you choose to work fulltime or part-time. About 19 percent of health care workers are on part-time schedules. In some areas, part-time work is even more common. About 38 percent of workers in dentists' offices are part-time. In doctors' offices, about 31 percent are part-time. One reason for the high overall number of part-time workers is many workers fill in only during busy times or work only part-time as a second job. Hospitals operate around the clock and need staff at all hours, so part-time work is also common in this area. Some part-timers work during the busy day periods,

Professional
Ethics

Accepting Gifts from Drug Companies

Health care workers at every level are constantly bombarded with advertising and promotion for drugs. Pharmaceutical sales representatives, also called *detailers*, hand out free pens, note pads, mouse pads, mugs, and just about anything else that can have a company logo on it. When detailers come to visit at the workplace, they often arrive bearing doughnuts or even lunch for the whole office. Detailers give out free drug samples to doctors; the drug companies are major sponsors of free training programs and seminars that can be used for continuing medical education. Is it ethically OK to accept these gifts? Some experts would argue that accepting anything, even a pen, from a drug company, is wrong, because it might influence you to use the company's product even if it is not the best choice for the patient. Others would argue that small gifts are so common that nobody is really influenced by them, so go ahead and accept that coffee mug. While drug samples can influence a doctor to start prescribing it, leading to more sales, doctors also give the samples to patients who cannot afford medicine. Things with greater value, such as an all-day seminar, are more of an issue. On the one hand, health care workers need to know about the latest drugs; on the other, many drugs are copycats and the goal of the seminar is really just to get you to use one brand over another. Adding to the confusion is that these seminars can often be counted toward your continuing medical educational requirement. Today more and more hospitals and medical centers have put limits on gifts from drug companies and other providers. If you are in doubt, refuse the gift and discuss it with your supervisor.

while others work in the evenings (often as a second job) or take night shifts a few nights a week. Shift work, including night shifts, is very common for health care workers, especially in hospitals. So is mandatory overtime, which can lead to shifts that last as long as 16 hours. And because people get sick on weekends and holidays, hospital workers and those in some other areas, such as emergency medical technicians, may be expected to work then too. Schedules in other settings, such as diagnostic labs or outpatient care centers, tend to be more regular and predictable. There is less opportunity for part-time work in these settings, however, and less opportunity for overtime and extra pay for working night shifts, weekends, and holidays.

Health care employers usually offer staff workers standard benefits such as health insurance, sick days, and vacation days. Part-time or hourly workers may not get the same package, however, and some employers do not offer benefits at all. On the other hand, some health care employers, particularly large medical centers, attract and keep skilled workers with generous benefits. Some offer tuition reimbursement, paid training, and flexible work hours.

Earnings by Area

Overall, hospital workers have the highest average earnings of all health care employees. In fact, according to the Bureau of Labor Statistic, average earnings of typical hospital workers are considerably higher than in private industry. The average weekly earnings for a hospital employee is $794; the average hourly earnings are $22. On average, hospital workers put in about 36 hours a week. Bear in mind that the numbers here are averages. In all areas of health care, workers with specialized training or certification can make considerably more than average.

Next highest on the earnings list are workers in medical and diagnostic laboratories. They make on average $715 a week or $19.50 an hour. They work harder than any other segment of the industry, putting in 37 hours a week on average.

Staff members in doctors' offices average $669 a week or $19.98 an hour. In outpatient care centers, average weekly earnings are $658 or $19.33 an hour. Dentist's office workers average $557 a week or $20.51 an hour. Most of these workers are part-timers—they average only 27 hours a week. Workers in other health practitioners' offices earn a bit less, averaging $498 a week or $17.27 an hour. They tend to have shorter work weeks as well, averaging 29 hours.

Workers in other ambulatory health care services, such as paramedics, average $555 a week or $15.58 an hour. They put in longer weeks, averaging 36 hours, not counting overtime.

Nursing home workers, residential care workers, and home health care workers are at the lower end of the earnings scale. The average home health care worker makes $429 a week or $14.78 an hour, and works 29 hours a week. In nursing homes and residential facilities, workers average $415 a week or $12.84 an hour and work about 32 hours a week. While staff workers may get benefits from their employer, many home health care aides do not, even when they work through agencies that place them with clients.

Earnings by Occupation

Another good way to look at earnings in the health care industry is by occupation. The numbers from the Bureau of Labor Statistics give a good overall picture of average earnings, but they can also be a bit misleading. Earnings tend to be higher for people who work in hospitals and large outpatient centers. They are also higher in some parts of the country, such as the Northeast, and in large cities nationwide. Many health care workers enjoy not only good pay, but also high job satisfaction. They work hard for their money and know that at the end of their shift they have made a difference in the lives of the people they help.

The earnings discussed below give an idea of the earning potential for some of the major health care areas. (Details of earnings for specific jobs will be discussed in Chapter 3.)

➡ Registered nurses. Nursing is one of the highest-paid areas in all of health care. In 2007, registered nurses earned on average $62,510 yearly or $30.05 an hour.

➡ Medical and health services managers. Management jobs in health care do not involve patient care, but they are vital for keeping health care establishments running smoothly and controlling costs. These jobs are highly paid, averaging $83,470 a year, or $40.13 an hour.

➡ Licensed practical and licensed vocational nurses. Earnings for licensed practical and licensed vocational nurses average $38,710 a year, or $18.61 an hour.

➡ Medical secretaries. Experienced medical secretaries earn $30,240 a year on average, or $14.54 an hour.

➡ Nursing aides, certified nursing assistants, and other attendants. Average yearly earnings for these workers are $23,660, or $11.37 an hour.

➡ Home health aides. These workers average $20,520 a year or $9.87 an hour.

The earnings outlook for health care workers is good. Salaries and hourly wages have shown steady rises over recent years. In some areas, demand for qualified health care workers is so high that employers pay bonuses to attract employees. They may also offer other incentives, such as free child care or tuition reimbursement.

Balancing pay increases are cost-cutting measures as hospitals, nursing homes, insurers, Medicare, and employers try to hold down rising costs. The upward income trend is still likely to continue, if more slowly, because of the increasingly high demand for health care workers. Going forward, workers with the most skills, such as nurses and radiology technicians, will continue to be sought after with good pay and benefits packages. Workers at the lower end, such as home health care aides, will probably find that hourly rates will not go up as quickly. Because these workers will be most in demand, however, pay is still likely to rise moderately in the coming years.

Today and Tomorrow in Health Care Employment

Even as workers in other areas are being laid off, job growth continues in health care. In 2009, for instance, the overall economy lost hundred of thousands of jobs and the national unemployment rate rose above 10 percent. But at the same time, the health care industry grew by 27,000 jobs. Only about 7,000 of those jobs were in hospitals. The rest—about 16,000—were in ambulatory care of various sorts. Layoffs and job freezes are very rare in health care, especially when most hospitals report that they cannot fill many of their nursing jobs and have many vacancies in other departments such as lab techs and CT scanner operators.

Health care seems likely to remain a strong part of the economy for years to come. The growth comes from a number of different factors:

→ An aging population. The huge baby boom generation is entering its 60s—the age when serious health problems, such as heart disease and cancer, start to be much more common. This very large bulge in the population will need plenty of health workers over the next few decades.

→ An unhealthy population. About a third of all Americans today are obese, which is a major risk factor for serious health problems such as heart disease, type 2 diabetes, some kinds of cancer, high blood pressure, stroke, liver and gallbladder disease, and arthritis, among other diseases. To take just one example, in 2009 some 23.5 million Americans have type 2 diabetes. Because diabetes can lead to heart disease, kidney disease, amputation, and blindness, in the years to come, these individuals will be frequent—and expensive—clients of all aspects of the health care system.

➡ An aging workforce. The average age of a registered nurse working in a hospital is 46.8. In 2004, the U.S. Department of Health and Human Services found that just more than 41 percent of RNs were 50 years of age or older. That is a big increase from 2000, when only 33 percent were over age 50. At the same time, only 8 percent of RNs were under the age of 30 in 2004. Though the numbers are less dramatic in other areas of health care, the heath care workforce is getting older and will need to be replaced as they retire. Workers entering the field will have more opportunities for promotion and leadership roles at a younger age.

➡ A shortage of spots in nursing schools and other training programs. Even though the demand for health care workers continues to rise, nursing schools have not been able to keep up. According to the Department of Health and Human Services, in 2004, nursing schools had to turn away more than 37,000 qualified potential students. Why? Because the schools did not have enough instructors, classroom space, clinical training sites, or mentors. Enrollment in basic RN programs increased from 181,415 in 2000 to 290,309 in 2006 and continues to rise slowly, but even this increase is not enough to fill the expected job openings. The same is true of other training programs, such as those for respiratory therapists.

➡ Cost containment. Of all the factors shaping health care going forward, cost containment will probably have the biggest impact. To save money, medical services are increasingly being provided on an ambulatory, outpatient basis at clinics and specialized treatment centers. As these centers grow, more workers will be needed. At the same time, patients in the hospital will be even sicker and will need more care from nurses, licensed practical nurses, certified nursing assistants, and a range of therapists. Cost containment will also eliminate some unnecessary or low-priority care, but the impact on jobs will probably not be large. At the management level, some jobs will be combined or streamlined to save salaries, but new jobs in health information technology will grow rapidly.

➔ Bigger hospitals. Over the coming years, smaller hospitals or those that are underused will be forced to close or merge to save costs. Larger hospitals, however, will continue to add beds and outpatient centers and will continue to need more workers in every area, including administration. Hospital growth will come from expanding regional medical centers and more specialty hospitals.

➔ Improved access to health care. Today some 49 million Americans do not have health insurance. Their access to health care is limited, leading to conditions that often go untreated. Efforts to reform the health insurance system and give all Americans access to affordable health care are likely to move forward in the future. Improved access to health care means more patients and more demand for health care workers and also for administrative help such as medical billers.

➔ Advanced technology. High-tech medical equipment such as dialysis machines for kidney failure and MRI machines for imaging need skilled technicians. As new, more sophisticated equipment replaces older technology, the strong demand for technicians will continue.

➔ Better treatments. All that advanced technology means doctors now have better ways to diagnose and treat health problems. That is good for all patients, but it is particularly helpful for trauma patients and the severely ill. The improved survival rates of these patients means they need extensive support from therapists and other workers as they recover.

➔ Electronic health records. A nationwide move to electronic health records for all patients means that there will be a large demand for information technology workers. Streamlining the health records system is a large and complex job. Current administrative workers will probably need some training or retraining to make the change, but any employee who's willing to learn the new systems will almost certainly still have work. The improved efficiency of electronic health records will be offset by the larger number of total records as access to health care improves. Job prospects in this area are very good.

The Major Players

The American health care system is huge, complex, often inefficient and inequitable, and very, very expensive. It is also very highly regulated by a confusing patchwork of federal and quasigovernmental agencies and national medical and professional societies. In addition, there are many industry associations that set quality standards and lobby at the federal and state level. On top of that, each state has its own department of health that regulates hospitals, nursing homes, and other facilities and sets licensing requirements for health care workers. What it all means is that there is a lot of overlapping responsibility and a certain amount of confusion as to who is in charge of what.

At the national level, the Department of Health and Human Services (HHS) is the government agency that sets most health care policy, creates most guidelines and regulations, and supports the most research and education. This huge department has many, many divisions. The most important for the day-to-day life of health care workers are:

➡ Food and Drug Administration (FDA). The FDA is responsible for approving all drugs and medical devices. A drug or device that does not have FDA approval cannot be legally sold or used in the United States. The FDA also regulates blood products, radioactive materials and machines such as PET scanners, contact lenses, lab tests, and many other materials and equipment used in health care. Being aware of FDA regulations is an important part of the job for many health care providers.

➡ National Institutes of Health (NIH). The NIH is the medical research and education arm of HSS. NIH scientists investigate ways to prevent disease as well as the causes, treatments, and even cures for common and rare diseases. The 27 institutes and centers that make up the NIH provide leadership and financial support to researchers in every state and throughout the world.

➡ Centers for Disease Control and Prevention (CDC). The CDC's mission is to protect the nation's health through promoting good health, preventing disease, injury, and disability, and preparing for new health threats. Among other activities, the CDC tracks infectious disease outbreaks. Some illnesses—such as salmonella (food poisoning), measles, and tuberculosis—must be reported to the CDC if they are diagnosed by health care workers.

➡ Centers for Medicaid and Medicare Services (CMS). Because Medicaid, Medicare, and State Children's Health Insurance Program (SCHIP) pay for a substantial part of health care in the United States, CMS is a crucially important agency. CMS sets reimbursement rates for anyone who provides services to Medicaid, Medicare, or SCHIP beneficiaries, including doctors, other health care providers, hospitals, nursing homes, medical labs, pharmacists, opticians, and many others. CMS also sets quality standards for every aspect of health care. Nursing homes and hospitals, for instance, must meet high standards to qualify for Medicaid/Medicare reimbursement. The same is true for outpatient care centers, medical laboratories, and even people who make artificial limbs. CMS also keeps a sharp eye on costs and looks for fraudulent activities by health care providers.

In addition to federal agencies, health care is governed by a number of quasigovernmental agencies—nonprofit organizations that are supported by the government but managed privately. These organizations set national standards and regulations.

➡ Institute of Medicine (IOM). The Institute of Medicine serves as adviser to the nation to improve health by providing independent, objective, evidence-based advice to policymakers, health professionals, the private sector, and the public. Among other things, the IOM sets the RDAs for vitamins and minerals.

➡ The Joint Commission. The full name of this important organization is the Joint Commission on the Accreditation of Healthcare Organizations. The Joint Commission evaluates and accredits more than 16,000 health care organizations and programs in the United States, making it the predominant standards-setting and accrediting body in health care. Keeping Joint Commission accreditation means continuously meeting high standards and quality improvement steps. Without the accreditation, an organization or program cannot get Medicaid, Medicare, SCHIP, or private insurance reimbursement and basically has to shut down. All accredited organizations spend a lot of time making sure they are meeting or exceeding the requirements and getting ready for their regular Joint Commission inspections.

➡ American Red Cross. We usually think of the American Red Cross as a disaster relief organization. That is a big part of what the organization does, of course, but from a health care perspective the Red Cross is most important for blood-related services. It provides whole blood for transfusions and blood products through 36 blood services regions. The high quality standards for handling blood set by the Red Cross are the standards followed by hospitals, blood banks, and drug companies across the country. The Red Cross sponsors blood drives across the country, often at hospitals and health care facilities. The Red Cross also sponsors first aid and cardiopulmonary resuscitation CPR training. Because passing these basic courses is often a requirement for getting a job, many, many health care workers have taken them and owe the first steps in their career to the Red Cross.

National professional associations and medical societies, such as the American Medical Association, American Nurses Association, American Academy of Family Physicians, Council of Medical Specialty Societies, American Physical Therapy Association, and many others help set national standards for their members. They set practice guidelines, ethical standards, and educational or certification requirements for their members. The practice guidelines of these organizations are set by panels of experts who have carefully studied the medical issues and come up with standardized recommendations for the best treatments. Practice guidelines are considered

Problem Solving

Improving Diversity in Health Care

The health care industry is not as diverse as the population it serves. Statistics from the Federal Health Resources and Services Administration (HRSA) show that today, about 87 percent of all registered nurses are white; about 5 percent are African American; 3.7 percent are Asian or Pacific Islander; and 2 percent are Hispanic. Minority nurses are high achievers. Among black nurses, 11 percent have masters or doctoral degrees, compared to 10 percent of white nurses. Nearly 10 percent of advanced practice nurses are from minority backgrounds, and 11 percent of nurse practitioners are minority nurses. To help bring minority students into health care training programs nationwide, HRSA has several programs that help colleges attract more students and minority faculty members and that offer grants to help disadvantaged students find the academic and financial support they need to graduate. Individual colleges and schools also work to attract minority students and help them succeed. Despite all the programs, there still are not enough minority workers in health care—the number of minority workers is lower than the overall minority population, a trend that will probably continue.

authoritative and guide how most patients are treated. Professional organizations also often define the scope of practice for their members—what a member can and cannot do in the treatment of a patient. Professional organizations also sponsor continuing medical education programs through in-person seminars and online and self-study courses. There is a professional society for just about every possible job title in health care. To get ahead in your career, join the one that is right for you. (More information about the importance of professional qualifications is in the On the Job and Tips for Success chapters.)

Nonprofit organizations that raise money and sponsor research and education about particular diseases are also important in health care. Some organizations, such as the American Heart Association, also set national care guidelines and quality standards that are used in hospitals and medical practices. Organizations such as the American Society for Clinical Oncology, the American Cancer Society, the March of Dimes, the National Breast Cancer Foundation, and literally hundreds of others all sponsor fund-raising and education activities. Health care workers are often asked to volunteer at these events. A modest amount of community volunteering is expected of health care workers, especially if the volunteer work uses your skills, like being a volunteer EMT at a bike-a-thon or an assistant at a blood drive.

Health care is a big industry, which means there are many industry associations. Most exist primarily to lobby at the federal and state level and to make sure their part of the industry is getting good publicity. They also run conferences, seminars, training programs, and other events to help professionals keep up with new developments. Some examples are the American Hospital Association, the National Alliance for Health Information Technology, and Pharmaceutical Research and Manufacturers of America (PHARMA).

Key Conferences and Industry Events

The health care industry is vast, varied, and broken into many segments. Not only that, ongoing medical research and new developments in every area of health care mean that there are more conferences and industry events in a week than most industries have in an entire year.

Most health care workers will want to attend or at least read about the events at national conferences that relate to their specialty training. If you are a nurse anesthetist, for instance, that could mean going to the annual meeting of the American Association of Nurse Anesthetists (AANA), where research papers are presented, vendors fill the exhibition hall, and job recruiters hold interviews. Almost all national health care associations have annual meetings, and many also sponsor multistate regional events and state and local events such as workshops that focus on new developments in a particular aspect of a specialty. A workshop sponsored by the American Physical Therapy Association (APTA) might focus on current thinking about treating back pain, for instance.

To find out about upcoming conferences and other events, check with the professional association for your specialty. Conferences are announced on the Web sites, in mailings to members, and in professional journals. Locally, your state professional association may hold conferences and workshops. For example, the New York State Association of School Nurses holds an annual conference and several other smaller events throughout the year. Many state, regional, and local events are sponsored by hospitals and other medical centers. A large regional hospital, for instance, might sponsor a day-long meeting on type 2 diabetes that would bring together doctors, nurses, health educators, and others from the community to discuss the latest ideas about treating these patients. State and even local meetings often have financial sponsorship from national organizations (the American Diabetes Association, for example) or from drug companies (such as those making drugs commonly used by people with diabetes).

Attending conferences, workshops, and training sessions is crucial for keeping up with developments in your specialty or skill. It is also a great way to network with colleagues and potential employers. Even at small or local conferences, hospitals and other employers often set up recruiting tables.

Large employers such as hospitals and outpatient care centers will often pay the conference registration fee and even travel costs and give an employee time off to attend. If you have any sort of health care license, registration, or certification, attending a conference can count toward continuing medical education requirements in your field.

Regulation of the Health Care Industry

No other industry in America is as heavily regulated at the federal, state, and even local level as health care. Meeting regulations and keeping up with changes is a major part of any health care job. While all that regulation may seem like a lot of extra work, it is designed to standardize procedures and keep patients, workers, and the public safe. For health care workers who deal with patients, a lot of regulations are just formal versions of common sense and good medical practices. At the administrative end, the regulations apply mostly to the confusing maze of billing and reimbursement from Medicaid, Medicare, SCHIP, and the many different private health insurers. It is no surprise that experienced workers trained in medical billing and insurance coding are in great demand.

At the federal level, many, many, many regulations apply to any health care organization that receives federal payment, particularly from Medicaid, Medicare, and SCHIP. Since almost every organization does receive this money in some way, federal regulations basically apply to everyone. As explained above, the Centers for Medicaid and Medicare Services (CMS), part of the Department of Health and Human Services, is the lead agency for most of these regulations, but many other federal agencies are involved as well, often with overlapping responsibilities. The Food and Drug Administration, for instance, regulates how drugs and medical devices are approved and also how they are used. At the same time, the Drug Enforcement Agency has some jurisdiction over how narcotic drugs such as morphine and oxycontin are prescribed.

Many other federal agencies also have regulations that apply to health care workers. The Occupational Safety and Health Administration, better known as OSHA, is part of the Department of Labor and is very important for health care regulation. OSHA's job is to set and enforce workplace health and safety standards and make sure that employers provide a workplace free of hazards that are likely to cause harm. OSHA sets the regulations, for instance, for how much radiation exposure a worker can have, and for how toxic materials and medical waste such as used needles need to be handled. A major role of OSHA is setting standards for preventing infection by blood-borne pathogens—germs that can cause illness if a health care worker is accidentally stuck by a needle or cut by a scalpel or other sharp object that was used on an infected patient. Diseases that can be passed on in this way include hepatitis B and HIV infection. All health care workers receive careful training on safe ways to handle *sharps*, the general term for needles and other sharp objects. Accidents still happen, but OSHA standards help keep the number down.

OSHA also sets standards for handling emergencies involving hazardous substances, such as a chemical spill. Every hospital is required to have a community emergency response plan that meets OSHA requirements. While this plan might never be put into action, creating it, training staff in it, and keeping it up to date are all major responsibilities for hospital administrators.

Some of the same issues that OSHA regulations cover are also covered by the federal Environmental Protection Agency (EPA), which is a department of its own. Strict EPA regulations apply to the disposal of medical waste, drugs, and radioactive materials, for instance, and some of these regulations overlap with OSHA regulations. Even the Department of Transportation (DOT) gets into the act by regulating exactly how medical waste has to be packaged and transported from the hospital or other facility to the disposal site— where the incinerator is regulated by the EPA but the workers fall under the jurisdiction of OSHA.

A final important area of federal regulation is the Health Insurance Portability and Accountability Act of 1996, better known as HIPAA. This law strictly regulates the privacy of records about a person's physical or mental health or health care. The law prevents the unauthorized disclosure of this information. The health care world takes HIPAA very seriously and goes to great lengths to protect patient privacy. This can lead to awkward situations for workers. A medical assistant at a busy doctor's office cannot call out a patient's full name when the appointment time arrives, because that would reveal the name to all the other people in the waiting room. Instead, he or she has to use just the first name, which some older adults find offensive, or use the first name and initial of the last name. HIPAA also means that health care workers need to be very careful about discussing patients in front of other people, such as in an elevator or over lunch.

Health care is heavily regulated at the state level as well. Licensing and regulation of health care professionals such as doctors, nurses, dietitians, physical therapists, and many others is generally done at the state level. The requirements for receiving and maintaining a license or certification vary from state to state. This leads to a 50-state patchwork of licensing requirements and creates headaches for the licensed or registered health care worker who wants to move to or work in another state. Credentials from one state are often but not always accepted by another. To help with this problem, a number of states have worked together to create the Nurse Licensure Compact. This agreement is among 22 participating states, including Texas, and allows anyone who is a registered nurse or licensed practical nurse/licensed vocational nurse in one state to work in any of the other participating states.

More and more health care workers are now required to have some sort of state licensing or certification. In 2008, for example, CMS began requiring certification for all kidney dialysis technicians. Although this is a federal mandate, the certification is issued by the states. To become a certified hemodialysis technologist or technician, however, applicants have to pass a standardized test given by any one of several different national professional societies, such as the

Nephrology Nursing Certification Commission. States can ask for more requirements on top of the test—some do, and some do not.

In addition to the formal certification needed for some jobs, health care workers often go on to be certified in a particular skill or medical specialty. These certifications are also based on national exams overseen by professional societies. Getting certified in something is very helpful for advancing your career. An EMT, for instance, might become certified in airway management or emergency cardiac care—steps that will also help him or her move up to being a paramedic. (Certification is so important to your health care career that it will be covered in detail in the job discussions in the On the Job chapter.)

Health care is a fast-moving area—new drugs, new treatments, new technology, and new problems arise constantly. Health care workers need to keep up with the changes. In fact, they are required to. Federal and state regulations say that all health care workers must take continuing medical education (CME) courses on a regular basis. The requirements vary depending on job title. As a general rule, the more advanced training and responsibility a worker has, the more continuing education is required. Nurse midwives, for instance, need to take more course hours and study more complex material than certified nursing assistants. To keep up with your continuing medical education requirements, check with your professional society. You can fulfill some CME requirements by going to a seminar or conference or doing a self-study or online program. Hospitals and other large employers often offer free in-service courses and training that can be applied to CME requirements; some employers will pay for you to attend classes. Teaching a class is also a way to fulfill CME requirements. Many health care workers use their mandatory continuing education to advance their careers by becoming certified in a new area.

Chapter 3

On the Job

Your job in health care is one part of a large and very complex system that has many different job titles with many different responsibilities. Because of that, health care can seem like a very fragmented business. Especially when you are thinking about health care as a career or you are in your first job, it can be hard to see how all the pieces fit together. Do not worry. The American health care system is so complicated that even the chief executive of a big hospital has trouble understanding what all her employees do and why she needs so many of them.

In this chapter we will explain what different workers in allied health care do, how their jobs fit into the larger picture, and where their careers can go. Every one of those jobs plays an important role in helping deliver quality health care to patients. While health care jobs can vary a lot in the level of training, responsibility, and pay, each and every job is important. Dr. Charles W. Mayo, the founder of the famed Mayo Clinic, once said, "There are no inferior jobs in any organization. No matter what the assigned task, if it is done well and with dignity, it contributes to the function of everything around it and should be valued accordingly by all."

One of the best things about a career in health care is that there are no dead-end jobs—if you are willing to put in the effort. Training and education are the keys to moving up. And because in many health care fields continuing education is usually also a state requirement for staying on the job, you can advance your career just by going to work. Even better, there is a good chance your employer will pay for some or all of your ongoing education. (Education opportunities are discussed in detail the Tips for Success chapter.)

Many health care jobs require some sort of certification. This is a complicated subject that will be discussed in the Tips for Success chapter. For now, bear in mind that certification usually means you have achieved a level of education and training that shows you are highly qualified in whatever career area you have chosen. This makes you more attractive to potential employers.

Associated Health Care Careers

Workers in associated health care provide nursing and other types of care directly to patients. They work very closely with doctors and often take over some medical functions so that the doctors can concentrate on patients with serious problems. Associated health care professionals have a high level of training. Under the supervision of a doctor, they are qualified to diagnose some medical problems and make treatment decisions for patients. This group of workers includes licensed practical nurses, registered nurses, dietitians, nurse practitioners, and physician assistants. In general, associated health care jobs offer the highest pay and most opportunities for moving ahead. All workers in this area, but especially registered nurses, are in high demand right now; demand will be even higher in the coming years.

Dietitian and Dietetic Technician Registered

There is an old saying, "Food is the best medicine." Dietitians would agree—it is their job to plan food and nutrition programs in a wide variety of health care settings. Hospitalized patients may need special diets to meet their nutritional needs. Dietitians make sure a patient with a feeding tube or serious burn injuries, for instance, is getting adequate nutrition. Clinical dietitians work with the medical staff in hospitals, nursing homes, and other facilities to coordinate care and make sure the patient is getting the best nutrition possible. In small institutions, a clinical dietitian may also manage the food services department, overseeing the kitchen workers and servers. Community dietitians work with individuals in outpatient settings such as health clinics and dialysis centers. They counsel patients on good nutrition and help with specific problems, such as weight loss or managing a health condition such as kidney disease or diabetes. Dietitians also train home health care workers in how to prepare nutritious food for children, the elderly, and people with special needs.

To become a registered dietitian, you will need a bachelor's degree in dietetics or a related area from a program approved by the Commission on the Accreditation for Dietetics Education (CADE). Many dietitians also hold a master's degree from an approved program. In addition to your coursework, you will need to complete 900 hours in an internship—this usually takes a year (two years if you do it part-time). You will then need to pass a national exam administered by the Commission on Dietetic Registration (CDR). Many RDs go on for advanced degrees and additional certification in specialized areas such as diabetes education.

An alternative career path is to become a dietetic technician registered (DTR). This credential means you have completed coursework in nutrition and have a two-year associate's degree from an accredited school. You have also done an internship lasting 450 hours and have passed a national exam administered by CDR. The DTR credential allows you to assist registered dietitians and even perform many RD functions. Right now, however, it is not a definite stepping-stone to becoming an RD—among RD programs, there is no standard for applying your DTR credentials to a bachelor's degree.

Fast Facts

What is the difference between a registered dietitian and a nutritionist? An RD has at least a bachelor's degree in nutrition or a related area and has passed a tough national exam. The term nutritionist is much more vague, and the educational requirements and training are generally not as well defined or demanding. Some states have laws that allow nutritionists to be certified or licensed–the requirements vary from state to state.

The job outlook for dietitians is fairly good. In 2006, about 57,000 people were working as registered dietitians. The Bureau of Labor Statistic projects that the need for dietitians will grow to 62,000, an increase of about 9 percent, by 2016. The demand will come mostly from the changing nutritional needs of an aging population. Jobs for dietitians and DTRs will be mostly in hospitals, nursing homes, rehab facilities, and outpatient treatment centers.

Average earnings for dietitians in 2009 were about $49,000 a year. For DTRs, the range is about $30,000 a year; many DTRs work on an hourly basis.

Licensed Practical Nurse

Licensed practical nurses (called licensed vocational nurses in Texas and California) provide much of the bedside care for patients in hospitals, nursing homes, and rehab centers. They work under the supervision of doctors and registered nurses. A licensed practical nurse (LPN) is usually responsible for basic patient care such as taking vital signs, giving injections, monitoring medical equipment, and changing bandages. They also help patients with bathing, dressing, eating, personal hygiene, and moving to and from the bed. Experienced LPNs often supervise nursing assistants and aides.

If you are currently a patient care worker such as a nursing aide, you could go on to study for the LPN or LVN qualification. Almost all LPNs and licensed vocational nurses (LVN) begin their career with a one-year, state-approved training program through a community college or vocational/technical school. Most programs require a high school diploma or the equivalent; some programs are part of the high school curriculum. LPN training combines classroom work with supervised clinical practice, where you work directly with patients. Completing the course successfully means you are eligible to take the national licensing exam, known as the NCLEX-PN. Every state requires LPNs to pass the exam. (In Texas and California some LVNs are excepted from the test.)

In 2009, there were about 719,000 working LPNs. About 19 percent were working part-time; the rest were fulltime workers, mostly in hospitals, nursing homes, outpatient clinics, and a variety of other residential health care facilities. Employment growth for LPNs is strong. The Bureau of Labor Statistics projects that an additional 105,000 LPNS will be needed by 2016, for a growth rate of about 14 percent. Most of the new jobs will be in nursing homes and other residential settings, but the largest demand will come in home health care. The aging population will have an increasing and long-term need for the sort of basic nursing care that LPNs provide.

LPNs and LVNs generally earn about $37,500 a year, usually as hourly workers. The average hourly wage for experienced workers is about $18. The highest pay for LPNs is in nursing homes, where the average hourly wage is $19.50. LPNs have good opportunities for overtime and extra pay for working nights, weekends, and holidays.

Becoming an LPN can be the first big step on a career ladder toward becoming a registered nurse. The LPN/LVN credential is usually accepted toward a nursing degree. Because LPNs bring a lot of practical experience to the classroom, they often do well, even if they have been out of school for a long time.

Registered Nurse

Nearly 2.5 million registered nurses are working today in health care. They are by far the largest group of health care workers—and there are not enough of them. Demand for nurses will continue to be very high. The Bureau of Labor Statistics estimates that another 587,000 nursing jobs will be created by 2016.

Most nurses—about 1.4 million of them—work in hospitals. About 209,000 work in doctors' offices and outpatient clinics; the rest work in various settings, including nursing homes and in home health care. No matter where they work, nurses have a lot of responsibility for patient care. They assess a patient's health problems and needs, develop and implement personalized nursing care plans, help perform diagnostic tests, operate medical equipment, and perform procedures for patients, such as inserting and removing catheters or intravenous lines. Nurses work under the supervision of doctors, but they are expected to make many decisions about patient care and to bring problems to the attention of the doctor. Perhaps most importantly, nurses advocate for their patients, making sure their care is a good and well-coordinated as possible. Particularly in hospital and nursing home settings, registered nurses supervise other health care workers, such as licensed practical nurses and certified nursing assistants.

Nurses can follow several different educational paths. Because medical care today is very complex, employers prefer nurses who have a four-year bachelor's degree from an accredited college—these nurses have the highest level of training. However, completing a two-year associate's degree program from an accredited program is perfectly acceptable for getting into the field. Many nurses go on to complete a bachelor's degree by going to school part-time—and sometimes an employer may help with tuition. Another way to enter nursing is through a diploma from an approved nursing program at a vocational school or training program. Here too, many nurses go on to earn degrees that will advance their careers. If you are currently an LPN or LVN, your credentials are a good step toward moving on to becoming a registered nurse.

After graduation, all nursing students must pass the national NCLEX-RN exam to become registered nurses. Passing the NCLEX-RN is a requirement for licensing in every state. In some states, that is all you need to become licensed, but requirements vary and in some states you may have to pass an additional exam.

Most nurses begin their career by working as a staff nurse in a hospital. As they gain experience, they often move into a specialized area that interests them, such as surgical nursing or working with premature babies. Nurses with experience and leadership ability can move up to supervisory positions, usually in a specialized part of the hospital, such as the intensive care unit, the cancer center, or the women's health clinic. Job titles here vary from hospital to hospital—unit manager, nurse manager, or nurse administrator are the more common names. Some nurses go on to become higher-level administrators within the hospital structure.

Registered nurses are encouraged to become clinical nurse specialists (CNS). These nurses have advanced expertise and training in a specific area of nursing, such as critical care or burn treatment, and usually hold master's degrees from accredited programs. Degrees and certifications are important for moving ahead on the nursing career ladder. Having solid credentials can lead to higher pay and an extra edge when applying for a promotion or a new job.

Registered nurses are among the highest-paid health care professionals. The average salary for an RN is $60,000, or about $29 an hour. Nurses with more training and experience or in specialized areas can earn more considerably more. The Bureau of Labor Statistics reports that the highest-earning nurses receive salaries of $87,000 or more a year, for an hourly wage of $42. Nurses can add to their earnings with overtime, night shift, weekend, and holiday pay.

Advanced Practice Nursing

Highly skilled nurses can go on for specialized training to become advanced practice nurses such as nurse practitioners, nurse anesthetists, and nurse midwives. The training usually leads to a master's degree and advanced certification or to a doctorate degree. Demand for advanced practice nurses is high. Their training allows them to perform more functions and procedures than RNs. This frees up the doctors to handle more complex and difficult cases. Advanced practice nurses always work under the supervision of doctors and can call on them for help at any time. Because their skills are in great demand, advanced practice nurses generally earn more than registered nurses.

Nurse Anesthetists

Certified registered nurse anesthetists (CRNA) administer anesthesia, drugs that make patients unconscious or insensitive to pain during surgical procedures. They also do pre-surgery exams, monitor the patient during the surgery, and take care of the patient after the operation is finished. Because there is a serious shortage of anesthesiologists (doctors who administer anesthesia), CRNAs fill the gap, especially in rural areas. About 37,000 CRNAs are practicing today, usually in hospitals, ambulatory surgery centers, and childbirth centers. Registered nurses who want to become CRNAs enroll in a program approved by the Council on Accreditation of Nurse Anesthesia Programs and study for anywhere from 24 to 36 months, including a clinical residency. At the completion of the program, they receive a master's degree and can take the certification exam given by the Council on Certification of Nurse Anesthetists (CCNA).

Nurse Practitioners

Nurse practitioners (NP) are trained to diagnose illnesses, treat injuries, order and interpret diagnostic tests such as X-rays and blood work, and, in some cases, prescribe medications. NPs also work closely with patients who have chronic illnesses such as diabetes to help them manger their health better. Today there are about 120,000 practicing NPs working in every sort of health care setting, including clinics, hospitals, nursing homes, and doctors' offices. To become an NP, you will need at least a four-year nursing degree and several years of experience as a nurse in a hospital or outpatient clinic. NP degree programs usually award a master's degree or, if you already have that degree, a post-master's certificate. More and more NP programs are awarding doctorate degrees. The programs combine classroom work with advanced clinical training. Today more than 325 colleges and universities offer NP degree programs; about 6,000 new NPs graduate every year. Licensing and certification requirements for NPs vary from state to state.

Nurse Midwife

Certified nurse-midwives (CNM) are registered nurses who have received advanced training in caring for women during pregnancy and childbirth. They usually work in hospitals and birthing centers and often care for women who have limited access to the health care system due to lack of health insurance or because they live in an area with few doctors. Certified nurse-midwives must graduate from a training program approved by the American College of Nurse Midwives; they receive a master's or doctorate degree, depending on the program. While CNMs are authorized to practice in every state, the licensing requirements vary considerably.

Physician Assistant

A physician assistant (PA) treats patients under the supervision of a doctor—in fact, PAs are formally trained do many of the things that doctors do. PAs take medical histories, examine and treat patients, order and interpret diagnostic tests such as X-rays and blood tests, and make diagnoses. They also perform minor medical procedures such as sewing up cuts and putting splints and casts on injured joints. In most states, PAs can also prescribe medications.

PAs usually work directly for physicians, helping with patients in the office and also caring for patients in the hospital or a nursing home. In rural and inner city areas where doctors are scarce, PAs may run clinics and provide basic medical care for the community even when a doctor is not present.

Many PAs start out as registered nurses. Others enter PA programs after graduating from a four-year college. Today 136 PA programs nationwide are accredited by the American Academy of Physician Assistants. Admission is very competitive and good grades in science and health-related courses are essential. Almost all PA programs are affiliated with a medical school or school of allied health. PA programs last for at least two years and usually lead to a master's degree. In addition to classroom and lab work, students do clinical training under the supervision of a physician. Graduates of approved programs must pass the Physician Assistant National Certifying Examination (PANCE), administered by the National Commission on Certification of Physician Assistants (NCCPA). In all states, passing the exam is a requirement for being licensed and for using the credential Physician Assistant Certified (PAC).

About 67,000 PAs are working today—and there is demand for many more. Employment for PAs is expected to grow 27 percent between 2006 and 2016. One reason is simply greater demand for health care, demand that doctors need help to meet. Another reason is cost containment. Treatment by a PA provides high-quality medical care for less. Salaries for PAs are high, ranging from $62,000 to $89,000 a year. The average PA earns $77,800 a year. According to the American Academy of Physician Assistants, even first-year PAs earn high salaries, averaging $69,000 a year.

Adjunctive Health Care Careers

Adjunctive health care workers are the many technologists, technicians, assistants, and aides who have specialized skills in a particular area. Many adjunctive health care workers operate complex

Fast Facts

Nursing Specialties

Most registered nurses specialize in one or more areas of patient care. The specialties fall into four general areas: _ Work setting or type of treatment. Nurses can work in settings such as critical care units, operating rooms, emergency rooms, cancer centers, hospices, and other specialized treatment facilities.

- Specific health conditions. Nurses in this area work with patients who have a particular health problem, such as cancer or diabetes.

- Specific body systems. Nurses in this area work with patients who have a disorder of a specific organ or body system, such as kidney disease or heart disease.

- Specific populations. Nurses in this area work with a defined group of patients, such as newborns, teens, or the elderly.

Nursing is very flexible and specialties often overlap. Some nurses specialize in working with children who have cancer, for example. By specializing, nurses become highly skilled and knowledgeable in their areas. In some areas, additional training and certification is needed, but often nurses learn their special skills on the job.

machinery such as CT scanners or dialysis machines; others are trained to perform specific functions, such as drawing blood or setting up an operating room for surgery. Others, such as nursing assistants, provide direct patient care at the bedside. As medical care gets ever more complex, adjunctive health care workers will be needed even more to operate equipment and provide patient care.

Job titles in adjunctive health care often contain the terms technician, technologist, assistant, hygienist, and aide. Although these positions are all lumped together as part of one career group, the education, responsibilities, and earnings can be very different. A high school diploma or the equivalent is needed for just about every job, but for most aide and assistant jobs, that is all you need to get started. To become a technician, you will need to complete a training program that could last anywhere from a few months to two years. For technologist jobs, a bachelor's degree is almost always a requirement. Many adjunctive jobs also require some sort of certification or licensing. Requirements vary from state to state—check the chapter Tips for Success for more detail.

Cardiovascular Technologist and Technician

Cardiovascular technologists and technicians work with doctors to help diagnose and treat cardiac (heart) and peripheral vascular (blood vessel) problems. They perform basic testing procedures, such as monitoring a patient's heart rate, recording heart activity using electrocardiograms (EKGs), administering stress tests, and using ultrasound equipment to visualize the heart and blood vessels. Some cardiovascular technologists are trained to assist in cardiac catheterization procedures. During a cardiac catheterization, a thin tube (catheter) is inserted into a blood vessel in the patient's groin and threaded up to the heart to see if there is a blockage in the blood vessels there and to treat the blockage if there is one. Cardiovascular technologists can also specialize in ultrasound procedures such as echocardiograms, which visualize the heart to show blood vessels and the heart valves. Using the same techniques, technologists can also visualize blood flow in other blood vessels elsewhere in the body, such as the carotid artery in the neck. Cardiovascular technicians assist in most procedures and can perform some, such as EKGs, on their own.

Most cardiovascular technologists learn their skills in a two-year program at a community college and have an associate's degree.

If you are already qualified in another area of health care, however, such as being a licensed practical nurse or a diagnostic medical sonographer, it is possible to complete the program in just one year. Currently, there are 31 accredited programs in cardiovascular technology. Students in diagnostic medical sonography programs (discussed later in this section) also learn cardiovascular skills and can apply for certification as a cardiovascular technologist. Certification as a cardiovascular technologist is offered by two organizations: Cardiovascular Credentialing International (CCI) and the American Registry of Diagnostic Medical Sonographers (ARDMS). Not every state requires a license for cardiovascular technologists; those that do usually also require certification. Even in states where certification is not required, many employers prefer it.

Cardiovascular technicians often learn their skills on the job, working under the supervision of a technologist or doctor. Many employers prefer to train people with some background in health care, such as nursing assistants. Short training programs that generally run for two to four months are offered at some community colleges and regional medical centers.

Half of all Americans will die of heart disease, and with an aging population the job outlook for cardiovascular technologists and technicians is very good. In 2009 about 47,000 people worked as cardiovascular techs. The Bureau of Labor Statistics estimates that employment will grow by 26 percent through 2016, to 57,000 workers.

Government salary and hourly wage statistics for cardiovascular technologists and technicians do not distinguish between the two. In general, technologists earn more because of their advanced training. The average salary is $46,000. In terms of hourly wages, at the low end, cardiovascular technologists/technicians earn about $12 an hour, while at the high end the hourly rate is about $35. The average is $22 an hour.

Dental Hygienist and Dental Assistant

When thinking about careers in health care, working in a dental office does not usually come first to mind. This is an area that tends to be overlooked, even though dentists employ more than 6 percent of all health care workers, mostly as dental hygienists and dental assistants. Dental hygienists perform a number of dental procedures on patients, including taking X-rays, examining the patient's teeth, gums, and mouth for problems, cleaning teeth, and educating patients on good oral hygiene.

Almost all dental hygienists work in dental offices under the supervision of a dentist. A distinctive feature of this health care profession is flexible scheduling. While some dentists' offices need full-time hygienists, many hire hygienists for part-time work. Evening or weekend hours are often available.

To become a dental hygienist, you will need to complete a two-year associate's degree program at a community college, technical school, or other program approved by the Commission on Dental Accreditation of the American Dental Association. Some 270 dental hygienist programs are currently accredited. Once you have graduated, you are eligible to take the National Board of Dental Hygiene certification exam. In most states, passing this test is required to be licensed as a dental hygienist. Once you get your state license, you are entitled to use the letters RDH, for registered dental hygienist, after your name.

Dental assistants work with dentists and dental hygienists to provide basic patient care such as taking X-rays, preparing patients for treatment, and scheduling appointments. The path to becoming a dental assistant varies quite a bit. Some dental assistants learn their skills on the job by working in a dental practice. Taking a short (usually nine to 11 months) training course at a technical school or community college gives you a more thorough background. Employers prefer to hire graduates of programs accredited by the Commission on Dental Accreditation of the American Dental Association. There are about 256 approved programs. Some states require certification by passing the national exam offered by the Dental Assisting National Board (DANBY). Passing the exam lets you use the letters CDA (certified dental assistant) after your name. It is also a good step toward admission to a dental hygienist program.

The job picture for dental hygienists and dental assistants is quite good. In 2009, nearly 169,000 dental hygienists were in practice. That number is expected to increase by 30 percent by 2016, or about 50,000 jobs, making dental hygienist one of the fastest-growing areas of health care. About 280,000 dental assistants held jobs in 2009. Here too job growth will be very high—an increase of 29 percent, or about 82,000 additional jobs, is expected by 2016.

Pay for dental hygienists is good. The average annual salary is close to $65,000; the average hourly wage is $31. Part-time workers earn less. Dental assistants are almost always hourly workers. The average hourly wage is about $14.50.

Diagnostic Medical Sonographer

Diagnostic medical sonographers use ultrasound (high-frequency sound waves) to produce images of organs, tissues, and blood flow in the body. Today ultrasound (also called sonography) is an important noninvasive diagnostic tool. It is used to image almost every part of the body, including the heart, the organs in the abdomen such as the kidneys, major blood vessels, and even the brain. Sonography is also used to examine women's breasts and to image the fetus in the womb of a pregnant woman. To create a sonogram, the sonographer uses special equipment to direct the sound waves into areas of the patient's body; the images are seen on a computer screen and are saved to the computer so that a doctor can look at them. The procedure is painless for the patient. More than half of all sonographers work in hospitals; most of the rest work in doctors' offices, outpatient clinics, and imaging centers.

Diagnostic medical sonographers usually start their careers with a two-year associate's degree training program at an accredited community college or technical school; some hospitals also offer accredited programs. A few colleges offer four-year bachelor's degree programs in sonography. About 147 programs are currently approved by the Commission on Accreditation for Allied Health Education Programs (CAAHEP). Health care workers with credentials in other areas, such as being an LPN or cardiac technician, can often move into sonography.

No state currently requires a license for diagnostic medical sonographers. A certification program is offered by the American Registry for Diagnostic Medical Sonography (ARDMS). Passing the national ARDMS exam, which includes a practical test of your ability to use the sonography equipment, allows you to be registered. This credential can give you an edge, because many employers prefer to hire registered sonographers.

In 2009, nearly 47,000 health care workers were diagnostic medical sonographers. The job outlook is good—the Bureau of Labor Statistics estimates that field will need about 19 percent more workers, or about 8,700 people, by 2016. The average annual salary for an experienced sonographer is about $60,000. On an hourly basis, the average pay rate is $29.

Emergency Medical Technician (EMT) and Paramedic

When someone calls 911 with a medical emergency such as a heart attack or accident, that is the first act in a chain response that will quickly send an emergency medical technician (EMT) or paramedic to help. As soon as the ambulance with the EMT or paramedic arrives on the scene, the first step is to provide immediate medical attention. That usually means assessing and stabilizing the patient and then transporting him or her to the nearest hospital. If the injuries are minor, the EMT or paramedic may simply provide first aid treatment on the spot. EMT and paramedics are trained to monitor vital signs and manage airway, heart, and trauma emergencies; paramedics are also qualified to administer drugs and perform some medical procedures, such as inserting a tube into the patient's airway to keep it open. All EMTs and paramedics are qualified to perform CPR.

About 40 percent of all EMTs and paramedics work for private ambulance services; another 30 percent work for local governments. About 20 percent work for hospitals, and the rest work in a variety of other areas, such as large industrial sites that have their own fire and emergency services. The work is physically demanding and can be very stressful. It often requires long shifts, overtime, and work on weekends and holidays. Challenging as the work may be, many EMTs and paramedics find that helping people or even saving a life is deeply satisfying.

EMTs are certified at two levels: basic and intermediate. The next step up is paramedic. Most EMTs start by taking a training course through a community college, vocational school, hospital, or public safety academy (usually a training facility operated by a state or municipality to train police officers, firefighters, and emergency medical workers). To become certified as a basic EMT (EMT-B) usually takes about 120 hours of training that combines classroom work with practical experience; the course ends with written and practical exams. Certification as an intermediate EMT (EMT-I) generally takes an additional 40 hours of training beyond the EMT-B level and also requires passing written and practical exams. Becoming a paramedic, also sometimes called EMT-P, usually takes considerably longer. Most paramedics train for at least 1,000 hours; some programs award an associate's degree for paramedics.

In all states, EMTs and paramedics must be certified by the National Registry of Emergency Medical Technicians. Additional certification and licensing, especially for paramedics, may be needed in some states. The state requirements vary quite a bit; you can usually find out more from the state's office of emergency medical services.

About 201,000 paid EMTs and paramedics are on the job. Growth in this area is projected to increase by 19 percent, or about 39,000 workers, by 2016. Earnings are somewhat variable, depending on your level of certification and location. In general, the average salary is about $31,000; the average hourly wage is about $15.

Hemodialysis Technician

Hemodialysis is used to remove normal waste products from the blood of people with kidney failure. The procedure uses a hemodialysis machine (an artificial kidney) that continuously pumps blood from the patient through filters that remove wastes; the cleansed blood is pumped back into the patient. Hemodialysis, often called "dialysis" for short, is a complex procedure, and it is performed on patients who are usually in poor health from the complications of kidney disease. These patients need careful monitoring while they receive treatment. That is where a hemodialysis technician comes in—he or she prepares patients for treatment, sets up, monitors, and cleans the dialysis equipment, and tends to the patient during treatment. Most hemodialysis technicians work in dialysis centers that are part of a hospital or are separate facilities. They usually work under the supervision of a registered nurse with a specialty in nephrology (kidney disease).

Until recently, most hemodialysis technicians learned their skills on the job or through a short training program offered by a hospital or dialysis center. In 2008, the Centers for Medicare and Medicaid Services announced that all hemodialysis technicians need to be certified. The goal is to create the same high standard of care at all hemodialysis centers nationwide. Because certification is now mandatory, many community colleges and vocational schools have started offering training programs. Most programs are fairly short, lasting about six to nine months going part-time; some more-intensive programs run for about 12 weeks. You must be a high school graduate or the equivalent to enter a program. Credentials in other areas, such as being a certified nursing assistant, can be helpful for getting accepted into a hemodialysis technician training program.

Certification for dialysis techs is currently offered by three different national programs. The Certified Clinical Hemodialysis Technician

(CCHT) certification is available from Nephrology Nursing Certification Commission (NNCC). The Board of Nephrology Examiners for Nursing and Technology (BONENT) and the National Nephrology Certification Organization (NNCO) also offer certification exams. So far, no one program seems to be more widely accepted than the others.

Certification for dialysis techs is so recent that reliable statistics about jobs are scarce. The job outlook for certified techs should be good, however. According to the American Kidney Foundation, every year more than 300,000 Americans need kidney dialysis. In 2009 there were about 3,200 for-profit kidney dialysis centers and another thousand or so operated by hospitals. Dialysis centers usually operate around the clock and need a lot of staff; evening, weekend, and holiday work is common. The average salary for a dialysis technician is about $27,000. Many dialysis techs are hourly workers—the average hourly rate for an experienced worker is about $16.

Home Health Aide

Home health aides, also called home care assistants, help care for people who need help in their homes to manage the activities of daily living, such as getting dressed, taking care of personal hygiene, eating, and taking medicine. They usually assist the elderly and the disabled, but they also often help people who are recovering at home from surgery, serious illnesses, or injuries. Home health aides help their clients stay independent and at home instead of needing to go to a nursing home.

Home health aides do not need to have a high school diploma or the equivalent, making this area very open to hard-working, reliable people without a good educational background. Most home health aides receive on-the-job training, usually along with some classroom instruction or workshops. If the agency you work for receives reimbursement from Medicare, you will have to pass a competency test that shows you can handle basic tasks such as washing your hands, helping a patient out of bed, and reading the medicine label correctly. To help you pass the test, most employers provide a short training course. Some states require home health aides to be licensed. The National Association for Home Care and Hospice offers voluntary certification for home health aides.

Earnings for home health care aides are low, often barely above minimum wage and rarely over $10 an hour. Most home health aides work a regular 40-hour week, but clients need weekend and sometimes need round-the-clock care. Weekend work is common, and you may have to do some evenings and holiday work as well.

Opportunities to get ahead are limited in this area, but experienced workers can become supervisors and help train new workers. Even if you did not have much educational opportunity or if English is not your first language, you can still learn skills such as first aid and CPR from local courses that are often free or cost very little. In fact, your agency may send you to these courses. The skills you gain make you a better aide and also give you an edge with employers. Some aides go on for additional training to advance in health care. They get the GED if they need it and go on to become certified nursing assistants or licensed practical nurses. Often the classes to get started are local and free or inexpensive. Your employer may even pay some costs or give you extra time off for the class as a way to keep a reliable worker with the agency.

The job outlook for home health care aides is extremely good. In part this is because the work is difficult and does not pay well, so there is a lot of turnover, but the demand mostly comes from an aging population that needs extra care. In 2006, there were 787,000 working home health care aides. The Bureau of Labor Statistics projects that by 2016, the need for these workers will reach 1,711,000—a growth rate of nearly 50 percent in just ten years.

Laboratory Technologist and Technician

Clinical laboratory technologists (also called medical technologists) and technicians examine and analyze cells and bodily fluids. Using microscopes and specialized equipment, they test specimens for bacteria, analyze the chemical content of blood and other fluids such as urine, test for drug levels, and perform many other tests and analyses that are crucial for diagnosing and treating health problems. Technologists are trained to perform more complex testing than technicians. All techs work in laboratories that are usually located in a hospital or at a private medical testing company. Most lab techs have little direct contact with patients.

Federal law requires that medical technologists have at least an associate's degree, but in fact most clinical laboratory technologists have a four-year bachelor's degree with a major in biology or medical technology. Additional training is provided on the job. Lab technicians usually have a two-year associate's degree from a community college or technical school. About 470 programs for medical laboratory technologists and technicians are approved by the National Accrediting Agency for Clinical Laboratory Sciences (NAACLS). Some states require lab workers to be licensed or certified, but this varies widely. Employers generally prefer to hire lab workers who are certified by one of several different agencies, including the Board of Registry of the American Society for Clinical Pathology, the American Medical Technologists, the National Credentialing Agency for Laboratory Personnel, and the Board of Registry of the American Association of Bioanalysts. No one certifying agency is strongly preferred over the others. Lab technicians work under the supervision of technologists and pathologists (doctors who specialize in laboratory work to diagnose illness) and do not require certification.

The job outlook for lab techs in general is moderately good. In 2009, there were about 163,000 clinical laboratory technologists. Growth here is projected at about 12 percent, for about 188,000 technologists by 2016. Lab technicians are also in moderate demand. About 146,000 technicians are working in labs. By 2016, that number is expected to rise to about 174,000, for an increase of about 15 percent.

Salaries for clinical laboratory technologists are good. The average tech earns about $52,000 a year; on an hourly basis, the average wage is $25. Lab technicians make about $36,000 a year, or about $17 an hour.

Nuclear Medicine Technologist

Nuclear medicine technologists are trained to perform diagnostic medical imaging that uses radioactive materials. For a PET (positron emission tomography) scan, for example, a tiny amount of radioactive material is injected into or swallowed by the patient. The scanning equipment then detects how the patient's body takes up the material and creates an image of that part of the body. If the patient has cancer, the radioactive material is taken up faster by the cancerous cells, and the image will reveal where the cancer is and how large it is. Nuclear medicine imaging is also used in some types of heart stress tests, to diagnose diseases of the thyroid and lymph glands, and for some other diagnostic purposes. Nuclear imaging is very safe for both the patient and the technologist.

Two-thirds of all nuclear medicine technologists work in hospitals. The rest work in outpatient centers, imaging centers, and in

Professional
Ethics

Reporting Suspected Problems

People who work in health care often see the physical and social signs of serious abuse problems, such as child abuse or sexual abuse. In fact, many health care workers, such as nurses, are now required to be trained in detecting and reporting abuse situations, especially child abuse. In most states, the law says suspected abuse must be reported. No matter what your job, if you think a patient is being abused in any way but cannot tell you or is afraid to come forward, bring the issue to the attention of your supervisor immediately.

Sexual harassment, drug and alcohol abuse, dangerous medical mistakes, mistreating patients, and other problems all happen in every health care workplace. If you see a problem, or if you make a medical error such as giving the wrong dose of a medication, report it to your supervisor *at once*. Your safety and the safety of your patients is at stake—do not hesitate to report errors and problems. To protect worker privacy and encourage honesty, many workplaces have procedures for reporting problems and medical mistakes anonymously.

doctors' offices (usually for heart doctors). Nuclear medicine technologists are highly skilled in using very complex, very expensive scanning equipment. Many nuclear medicine technologists get their training through a four-year bachelor's degree program. Some are trained through two-year associate's degree programs at community colleges or technical schools. Health care workers with degrees or accreditation in other fields, such as radiologic technicians or diagnostic medical sonographers, can usually move into nuclear medicine by doing a one-year certificate program. Whichever route you choose, select a program that is accredited by the Joint Review Committee on Education Programs in Nuclear Medicine Technology. In 2009, there were only about 110 accredited programs nationwide.

More than half of all states currently require nuclear medicine technologists to be certified or licensed. Other states are likely to begin requiring certification or licensing within the next few years. Certification is available from two agencies: the American Registry of Radiologic Technologists (ARRT) and the Nuclear Medicine Technology Certification Board (NMTCB). The certification requirements differ somewhat between the two, but both require passing a comprehensive exam. Employers in this area definitely prefer certified workers.

In 2009, more than 20,000 nuclear medicine technologists were employed. That number is expected to grow to about 23,000 by 2016, for an increase of about 15 percent. Experienced nuclear medicine technologists earn an annual salary of about $65,000; on an hourly basis, they usually make about $31. Nuclear medicine techs work fairly regular hours, but they are usually expected to work at least one weekend a month and may also be expected to work evenings and on holidays.

Patient Care Worker, Nursing Aide, and Certified Nursing Assistant

Patients in hospitals, nursing homes, and rehab facilities need a lot of help with ordinary activities, like getting in and out of bed, personal hygiene, getting dressed, and eating. Patients also need to be monitored for vital signs, given their medicine, and be escorted to and from treatment areas. These tasks are done by patient care workers. In hospitals and rehab centers they are usually called nursing aides, nursing assistants, attendants, orderlies, patient care associates, or patient care aides. In nursing homes, certified nursing assistants provide most of the day-to-day care. Patient care workers usually work under the supervision of a licensed practical nurse or registered nurse.

Patient care work is physically demanding—you are on your feet a lot and often have to lift or support patients. Night shifts and weekend and holiday work are expected—which makes patient care work a good option for second or part-time jobs. In fact, about 23 percent of all patient care aides work part-time, compared to 15 percent of all workers. If you are thinking of a career in health care, patient care work is a good way to get a feel for what goes on in a hospital and what your future job might involve.

Entry-level work as a patient care provider requires a high school diploma or the equivalent. In most states, employers must run background checks and drug tests on potential employees. New workers usually learn their skills on the job. Employers such as hospitals and nursing homes often offer a short training course (two to six weeks) that teaches basic patient care, infection control, proper lifting techniques, and other important skills. You will probably be paid while you take the course, usually in exchange for an agreement to work at the facility for a fixed time after the course is over. Short courses are also offered at community colleges and vocational schools and sometimes through a local Red Cross chapter.

The process is similar for becoming a certified nursing assistant (CNA), but the training part can last for as long as six months, especially if you study at a community college or vocational school. Certification requirements vary from state to state, but always involve both a written exam and a practical test of your patient-care skills. Federal law says nursing assistants in nursing homes must be certified. Today the CNA credential is in demand, because you can be hired by a nursing home and start working with residents immediately under the supervision of a registered nurse. The CNA credential is a requirement to provide patient care in a nursing home. Although it is not a requirement for doing similar work in a hospital, it shows you already have training in basic skills and would give you an edge in being hired. The CNA is also a good starting point for going on to become a licensed practical nurse.

Patient care workers are currently in high demand, in part because the work is difficult and not for everybody—there is a lot of turnover. Because of an aging population that will spend more time in hospitals and nursing homes, demand for patient care workers is expected to be very high in the future. In 2006, about 1.45 million people were working as patient care providers. By 2016, that number will grow to 1.7 million, an increase of about 264,000 workers.

Despite the high demand, patient care workers are at the low end of the health care pay scale. The hourly wage ranges from around $9 to $12. Pay rates for CNAs are somewhat higher. The hourly wage ranges from $10 to $15. Overtime and extra pay for working on weekends and holidays can add to earnings.

Pharmacy Technician

Pharmacy technicians help registered pharmacists dispense medication and other health care products to patients. They help with much of the routine work in a retail pharmacy, such as counting out pills and taking payment at the cash register. About 71 percent of pharmacy techs work in retail settings, usually in drugstores and in the pharmacy sections of grocery stores and large retailers. Pharmacy technicians also work in hospitals and nursing homes, usually preparing medications and delivering them to patients—always under the supervision of a pharmacist. Being a pharmacy tech in a hospital gives you a good look at other health care jobs. Your experience as a pharmacy tech can be a steppingstone to becoming a patient care worker, certified nursing assistant, or LPN.

Most pharmacy technicians learn their skills on the job. Currently there are very few federal or state regulations covering pharmacy techs. Some community colleges and vocational schools offer training for pharmacy technicians; the course may provide a certificate or associate's degree. Pharmacy techs can also take a national certification exam from either the Pharmacy Technician Certification Board or the Institute for the Certification of Pharmacy Technicians. In some states, the certification may be mandatory. Even if it is not, employers much prefer to hire certified workers, because they know they do not have criminal records or a history of drug use—issues that are of special concern in pharmacies.

In 2009, about 302,000 people were working as pharmacy technicians. Growth in this area is expected to be high. By 2016, 376,000 pharmacy techs will be needed, an increase of 74,000 workers. Almost all pharmacy techs are hourly workers; the average hourly wage is about $13. Many jobs in this area are part-time; evening, night, weekend, and holiday work is common.

Radiologic Technologist and Technician

Radiologic technologists are the health care professionals who operate diagnostic imaging equipment such as X-ray, MRI, and CT machines. They help prepare patients for imaging and are also responsible for maintaining the equipment. Some radiologic technologists (also called radiographers) specialize in a particular type of equipment or in a particular area, such as mammography. Most radiologic techs (about 60 percent) work in hospitals. The rest mostly work in outpatient clinics, imaging centers, and doctors' offices.

To get into this field, most radiologic technicians complete a two-year associate's degree program at a community college or technical school accredited by the Joint Review Committee in Radiologic Technology. Most states now require licensing for radiologic technologists.

A first step toward a license is certification through a national exam given by the American Registry of Radiologic Technicians (ARRT). As new and more advanced imaging machines become available, radiologic techs have more opportunities for training in how to operate the equipment. Learning new skills in this area can lead to additional certification through the ARRT.

According to the Bureau of Labor Statistics, about 200,000 radiological techs were on the job in 2009; an estimated 26,000 more techs will be needed by 2016. Radiological technologists usually work a regular 40-hour weeks, but some evening, night, weekend, and holiday work is usually part of the job. Part-time work and shift work is fairly common in this area.

According to the ARRT, the average salary for an experienced radiological technologist is $47,000 a year. Specialists who work with CT or MRI equipment usually earn more, up to $60,000 or even more. On an hourly basis, radiological techs generally earn about $25.

Surgical Technologist

Also known as scrubs, surgical technologists work as part of a medical team to assist during surgical operations. They help prepare the operating room before and after surgery, help prepare and transport patients, and help the surgeon during the operation. With additional training, surgical technologists are allowed to operate some equipment and assist the surgeon with some procedures. About 70 percent of all surgical technologists work in hospitals, usually in operating and delivery rooms. The rest work in ambulatory surgery centers and in doctors' offices. Most scrubs have a regular workweek, but some evening, night, holiday, and weekend work may be required.

Most surgical technologists learn their skills through a program at a community college or vocational school accredited by CAAHEP. Some courses are as short at nine months; others take two years and grant an associate's degree. Surgical technologists do not have to be licensed or certified, but employers prefer graduates who have passed the national certification exam offered by the Association of Surgical Technologists. Passing the exam lets you use the letters CST (certified surgical technologist) after your name. If you already have a credential as a certified nursing assistant or LPN, you may have an edge in admission to a surgical technologist training program.

Fast
Facts

Telling the Doctors Apart

In a hospital, a lot of people who do different things are all called doctor. Here is who's who:

- Attending physician. A medical doctor who is in charge of a patient's treatment. An attending, as he or she is often called, might also supervise a team of medical students, residents, and fellows.

- Fellow. A fellow is a doctor who has graduated from medical school, completed a residency, and is now training in an advanced medical specialty such as heart surgery.

- Resident. A resident is a doctor who has graduated from medical school and is now training in a specific field, such as pediatrics. Doctors spend anywhere from three to seven years in residency training. They are closely supervised by attending physicians who must approve their decisions.

- Doctorate degree holders. Many advanced health care workers, including nurses, physical therapists, social workers, and others, hold doctorate degrees and are entitled to be addressed as doctor.

Tip: You can tell the doctors from the medical students by their white coats. Students wear short coats that end at the waist; doctors wear longer coats.

In 2009, there were about 86,000 working surgical technologists. Demand in this area is very high, because an aging population needs more operations. By 2016, an additional 21,000 surgical techs will be needed. The average salary for an experienced surgical technologist ranges from about $32,000 to $40,000. On an hourly basis, the average wage is about $18.

Rehabilitation Health Care Careers

Rehabilitation workers in health care are trained professionals who help patients recover from surgery, injuries, strokes, and other health problems that can impair normal function. They also help people with disabilities maintain and improve their normal functioning. In all cases, the goal is to help patients regain their ability to perform all the activities of daily living and stay independent.

Audiologist

Audiologists work with people who have hearing, balance, and other ear-related problems. They help patients learn to use hearing aids and other devices and help them learn communication skills to compensate for poor hearing. Audiologists usually work in doctors' offices, outpatient clinics, or in private practice; some work in patients' homes through a home health care agency. Most audiologists have a standard five-day workweek.

Audiologists must have at least a master's degree and preferably a doctorate degree in audiology (AuD) from a program approved by the Accreditation Commission on Audiology Education or the Council on Academic Accreditation in Audiology and Speech-Language Pathology (CAA). In all, there are only about 130 graduate programs in audiology nationwide. In every state, audiologists must be either licensed or registered. The requirements vary widely from state to state. In many cases, the Certificate of Clinical Competence in Audiology (CCC-A) offered by the American Speech-Language-Hearing Association is required. Certification from the American Board of Audiology may also be accepted for licensing or registration.

In 2009, about 11,300 audiologists were on the job. Job growth in this area is moderate—about 13,000 audiologists will be needed by 2016. Salaries for audiologists range from about $47,000 to about $70,000 a year; on an hourly basis, the average wage is about $30.

Health Educator

Encouraging a healthy lifestyle and helping people prevent diseases and other problems are the primary goals of health educators. They organize classes, lectures, support group, workshops and other types of programs to teach the community about good nutrition, exercise, quitting smoking, breast self-exams, and many other health topics. They may also help individual patients with a particular disease, such as diabetes, learn how to manage their condition.

Health educators work in a very wide variety of fields. About half work in health care—usually in hospitals, outpatient clinics, and nursing homes—and for social assistance agencies. Another 20 percent or so work in public health for local, state, and federal governments. The rest work for nonprofit agencies, in schools and colleges, for companies, and in other areas.

Becoming a health educator usually requires at least a bachelor's degree in health education. More than 250 colleges offer this degree. To move ahead, a master's degree is almost always needed. Graduate programs in health education are numerous and varied and may focus on a specific area, such as school health education. A background in other areas, such as nursing, is often acceptable for admission to a master's program. Some health educators may decide to become Certified Health Education Specialists by passing an exam offered by the National Commission of Health Education Credentialing, Inc. In some states this certification is needed to work for a public health department.

The job outlook for health educators is very good, mostly because insurers are looking for ways to hold down costs by preventing illness through better education. Employment in this area is expected to rise from about 62,000 workers in 2006 to 78,000 in 2016, an increase of 16,000 people. Salaries in this area range from about $31,000 for entry-level workers to $56,000 or more for experienced workers with graduate degrees.

Occupational Therapist and Occupational Therapy Assistant

Occupational therapists work with patients who have physical, developmental, mental, or emotionally disabling conditions. They help these patients improve their ability to do all the ordinary activities of daily living and to function better in the classroom or workplace. Often the work involves teaching a patient with a disability how to perform a basic skill, such as getting dressed, or how to use adaptive aids such as wheelchairs and communication devices. OTs also help elderly clients stay active and independent—for example, by teaching them skills to keep them driving safely and training them in fall prevention.

Most occupational therapists work in hospitals, outpatient clinics, and residential centers. Some work for agencies and make house calls on clients. In general, OTs have a standard workweek and do not usually need to work on weekends or evenings. More than 25 percent of occupational therapists are part-time workers. Ninety-one percent of occupational therapists are women.

To become an occupational therapist, you will need to have a bachelor's degree, preferably in a health-related field, and then earn a master's or doctorate degree through a program approved by the American Occupational Therapy Association (AOTA). Competition for graduate programs is strong—there are only about 124 approved OT programs nationwide. To complete your degree, you will need to do six months of supervised fieldwork. Every state requires occupational therapists to be licensed. As part of the licensing process, you will need to pass the national certifying exam given by the National Board for Certification in Occupational Therapy (NBCOT). If you pass, you can use the letters OTR (Occupational Therapist Registered) after your name.

Occupational therapists are in high demand. In 2009 there were about 92,000 working OTs. By 2016, the nation will need 122,000 occupational therapists, or 30,000 additional workers, to help with an aging population and a greater need for services to schoolchildren.

Occupational therapy assistants (OTA) help OTs with patient care by preparing the treatment area, escorting patients, helping with treatment, and assisting with paperwork and other routine work. To become an OTA, you will need to complete an approved two-year associate's degree program at a community college or vocational school. In most states, you will need to be certified by passing the national certifying exam given by NBCOT. If you pass, you are entitled to call yourself a COTA (Certified Occupational Therapy Assistant).

Experienced occupational therapists generally earn between $55,000 and $65,000 a year. Occupational therapy assistants earn salaries in the range of $35,000 to $40,000 a year.

Physical Therapist and Physical Therapy Assistant

Physical therapists (PT) are health care professionals who help patients reduce pain and regain or improve their ability to move and perform the activities of daily living. They work with patients who have medical problems, disabilities, or who are recovering from injuries. Treatment by a PT often includes strength, balance, and coordination exercises; stretching, and teaching patients how to use assistive devices such as crutches, wheelchairs, and artificial limbs.

About 20 percent of physical therapists work in hospitals. The rest work in a wide variety of settings, including outpatient clinics, rehab facilities, nursing homes, and fitness centers. Most PTs work a regular week and rarely have weekend or evening hours. About 20 percent of PTs currently work part-time.

Training to become a physical therapist takes a long time. A PT needs at least a master's degree, and increasingly training programs are moving toward the doctor of physical therapy (DPT) degree. Most physical therapists have a bachelor's degree in a health-related or science field. They go on for a master's or DPT degree at a program accredited by the American Physical Therapy Association (APTA). In 2009 there were about 200 accredited programs, and admission is very competitive. To get a master's degree in physical therapy usually take two years. A doctorate can take three years or longer. Every state requires licensure of physical therapists. At a minimum, to get a state license PTs have to pass the National Physical Therapy Examination (NPTE), administered by the Federation of State Boards of Physical Therapy (FSBPT).

Physical therapy assistants (PTA) help physical therapists provide treatment to patients. They help patients exercise and learn to use assistive devices, keep the treatment area clean and prepared for patients, escort patients, and help with clerical work. To become a physical therapy assistant, you will need an associate's degree from a community college or technical school from an accredited PTA program; there are currently about 234 programs nationwide. In most states, PTAs need to be licensed, registered, or certified. The first step is passing the FSBPT's National Physical Therapist Assistant Exam. Being a PTA may give you an edge in applying for a bachelor's degree program in a health-related area and then possibly moving on to becoming a PT.

Physical therapists are in such demand that there is virtually no unemployment among them. About 162,000 PTs were working in 2009; another 58,000 will be needed by 2016. Physical therapy assistants are also badly needed. In 2009, there were about 60,000 on the job; by 2016, the Bureau of Labor Statistics projects that 20,000 more will be needed.

According to APTA, the average salary for an experienced PT in 2009 was around $75,000. For experienced PTAs, the average salary is around $42,000.

Radiation Therapist

The primary job of a radiation therapist is treating cancer patients. Radiation therapists work as part of a medical oncology (cancer) team. They operate equipment that aims radiation from a liner accelerator directly to the patient. The radiation beam is very targeted so that it hits only the area with cancer and avoids healthy parts of the body as much as possible. As part of the treatment process, radiation therapists also use X-ray and CT machines to pinpoint exactly where to aim the radiation. Although radiation therapy does have side effects for the patient, it is very safe—and it is also very safe for the radiation therapist.

Radiation therapists usually work in hospitals, cancer centers, and outpatient radiation therapy facilities. They usually have a standard workweek, although it may start very early to accommodate patients who will receive their therapy and then go to work.

Radiation therapists usually have associate's or bachelor's degrees in radiation therapy from a program approved by the American Registry of Radiological Technologists (ARRT). In 2007, there were 123 approved programs. Some states require licensure for radiation therapists. The first step toward licensure is passing the national certifying exam from the ARRT; even in states that do not require licensure, certification is almost a necessity. As new and more complex machinery comes into use, radiation therapists will have more opportunities for additional training in specialized areas.

Radiation therapy is a small field compared to other areas of health care. In 2009, there were only about 14,600 certified radiation therapists. Demand will increase in the coming years as the number of patients with cancer grows, radiation technology improves, and older workers retire. The Bureau of Labor Statistics estimates that by 2016, 18,000 radiation therapists will be needed.

Salaries for radiation therapists are good. In 2009, an experienced radiation therapist earned anywhere from about $55,000 to $78,000 a year. Salaries were highest at outpatient care centers.

Respiratory Therapist and Respiratory Therapy Technician

Respiratory therapists treat patients who have breathing or lung problems due to illnesses such as asthma, emphysema, or heart failure, or because of an injury or disability. Working closely with doctors, RTs treat everyone from premature babies with breathing problems to elderly people with lung disease, including patients who need life-support such as ventilators to breathe. They also evaluate patients and do diagnostic breathing tests, provide oxygen therapy, and teach patients how to use oxygen equipment and inhalers. Because respiratory problems are so common, respiratory therapy is a major area

INTERVIEW

Why I Love Being a Speech Language Pathologist

Lara Simmons, MS
Speech therapist, Kingston, New York

What got you interested in speech-language pathology?

When I was in high school, I had a vague idea that I wanted to be some sort of therapist. I went to a small liberal arts college, though, and it did not have any therapy programs. I ended up being an American history major. After I graduated, I had a couple of jobs working for nonprofit organizations, but I did not feel my career was going anywhere. A good friend was studying to become a speech language pathologist at a nearby state university. She was so enthusiastic about it that I got interested, too. I took a leap of faith and decided to apply to the same program. I had to do a year of prerequisites first. I never studied so hard—and it paid off when I was accepted to the master's degree program. I was really amazed when I started my degree to learn about all the different things a speech pathologist does and what the career possibilities were. After two years of really hard work, including 350 hours of internship, I was ready to do my clinical fellowship year at a local hospital. I worked with all sorts of patients, ranging from tiny kids to seniors. It was a great experience. It taught me that we take our ability to speak for granted until we lose it. It gives me great satisfaction to help my clients learn to speak more clearly and to regain lost speech ability.

Where has your career taken you?

In my career so far I have worked at a hospital for several years, for an agency for several years, and now at a nursing home, where I mostly help the residents with swallowing problems. The great thing about being a speech pathologist is that there are always interesting jobs out there. If you get burned out by working in one area, you can move into another. I feel very fortunate to work in a part of health care that I love and where my skills are in high demand.

of health care—about 101,000 respiratory therapists are currently on the job. Respiratory therapy technicians work under the direction of a respiratory therapist or a doctor. They assist with treatment, escort patients, prepare and clean equipment, and help with paperwork. This job title is less common—about 18,000 RTAs were working in 2009.

Most respiratory therapists and respiratory therapy technicians work in hospitals. Some work in outpatient care centers, nursing homes, rehab centers, and for agencies that send them on home visits to patients. Most RTs have regular hours, but some evening, night, weekend, and holiday work may be required. Respiratory therapists and technicians often work part-time second jobs in the field, usually for home care agencies.

To become a respiratory therapist, you will need at least an associate's degree from a program approved by the Committee on Accreditation for Respiratory Care (CoARC). To become a respiratory therapy technician, you will need to complete at least a one-year program approved by CoARC. In 2009, there were nearly 400 approved programs nationwide. In almost every state, respiratory therapists and respiratory therapy technicians need a license to practice. To be licensed as either, you start by meeting the requirements for becoming a Certified Respiratory Therapist (CRT) of the National Board for Respiratory Care (NBRC), including taking the national exam. To become a respiratory therapist, you must go on to take two more exams from the NBRC, leading to the credential Registered Respiratory Therapist (RRT), which is a requirement for state licensing.

In the years to come, rapid growth in the need for both respiratory therapists and respiratory therapy technicians is expected. The Bureau of Labor Statistics projects that by 2016, the nation will need some 126,000 respiratory therapists, an increase of about 25,000 workers. Projections for respiratory therapy technicians are not available, but in general this area can be expected to grow as well.

Salaries for respiratory therapists are fairly good, averaging around $50,000 a year for experienced workers. On an hourly basis, pay ranges from about $17 an hour up to about $25 an hour. For respiratory therapy technicians, salaries are in the $30,000 to $40,000 range; hourly work is in the range of $16 to $24.

Speech-Language Pathologist

A speech-language pathologist, also sometimes called a speech therapist, is a health care professional who helps clients with problems related to speech, language, voice, swallowing, and communication due to development disorders, injuries, surgery, stroke, hearing loss, and many other reasons.

About half of all speech-language pathologists work in preschools and schools helping children. The rest work in hospitals, nursing homes, outpatient clinics, and as contract workers for agencies that provide home health care services. Almost all have a standard five-day workweek.

Speech-language pathologists must have a master's degree from a program approved by the Council on Academic Accreditation in Audiology and Speech-Language Pathology (CAA) to enter the field. There are more than 230 approved master's programs; they include classroom work, supervised fieldwork, and an internship lasting at least nine months. In almost all states, speech-language pathologists must be licensed or registered. Passing the Praxis Series exam offered by the Educational Testing Service is necessary for licensure or registration. In some states, the Certificate of Clinical Competence in Speech-Language Pathology (CCC-SLP) offered by the American Speech-Language-Hearing Association can substitute for the Praxis exam.

In 2006, about 110,000 people were working as speech-language pathologists. About half worked in preschools and school. The rest worked in hospitals, outpatient clinics, nursing homes, doctors' offices, and in patients' homes through home health care agencies. Although growth in this area is expected to be about average, employment prospects are excellent. In the educational area, increased services for children with disabilities means high employment in school settings. The aging population will have increased problems with speech, language, and swallowing, and will need more treatment from speech-language pathologists. By 2016, 121,000 speech-language pathologists will be needed, an increase of 12,000 over 2006.

Earnings for speech-language pathologists range from about $50,000 a year to over $70,000 for experienced professionals. The average hourly wage is about $31.

Administrative Careers

Delivering quality health care takes a huge amount of administration and back-office work. A lot of jobs in this area do not require special health care training and have little or no contact with patients. Someone in the accounts payable department, for instance, needs good training as a bookkeeper but not any special training in hospital procedures—that is learned on the job. Some administrative areas in health care, however, are special skills that need special training, especially if they involve working with patients and health care providers such as doctors and nurses.

Health Information Technician

Every time a patient has any contact with the health care system, records are generated. Often called "charts," a patient's medical records can be extensive and involve the input of several different doctors and many other health care providers as well. The amount of paperwork charts create is vast. So is the confusion, duplication, delay, and extra costs caused by lost or inaccurate records, or simply because a doctor's handwriting is hard to read. More and more, the health care field is adopting the practice of electronic medical records (EMR) to control costs and help prevent medical errors.

Health information technicians (IT) assemble patients' health information into EMRs and make sure they are accurately entered into the computer system. They add information and updates to the patient's record as needed and consult with doctors and other health care professionals to solve problems or obtain additional information. Some health ITs specialize in working with cancer registries, where patients are tracked over years to see what happens to them.

Health information technicians work in the administrative offices of hospitals, outpatient clinics, cancer treatment centers, doctors' offices, nursing homes, rehab centers, and anywhere else that provides treatment to patients. About two of every five health IT jobs are in hospitals.

Some health IT workers learn their skills on the job, usually starting as medical assistants who are responsible for patient records and learning additional skills through short training courses, online programs, and workshops. As the field has grown and become more complex, however, getting ahead—or even entering health IT—often now requires special training. Employers look for workers with an associate's degree from a community college or technical school or through distance learning, preferably through a program accredited by the Commission on Accreditation for Health Informatics and Information Management Education (CAHIIM). The coursework usually includes medical terminology, legal and confidentiality issues, database management, computer skills, and quality improvement methods. Employers prefer to hire health IT workers who have passed the written exam offered by the American Health

Information Management Association (AHIMA). Only graduates of the 250 or so CAHIIM-approved programs are eligible for the exam. If you pass, you can use the credential Registered Health Information Technician (RHIT).

Job prospects for workers in health information technology are extremely good. A major national effort to computerize all health records is creating many opportunities for employment in the field. So is the growing movement among consumers to place their medical records online. The Bureau of Labor Statistics predicts the workforce in this area will grow from 166,000 in 2007 to 200,000, or 34,000 more workers, in 2016. This may be an underestimate—job growth could well be much higher. A 2009 study in the *New England Journal of Medicine* found that only 13 percent of doctors' offices had a basic EMR system in place and that only about 10 percent of hospitals have an EMR system.

Salaries in this area are on the low side, especially for entry-level workers. The average salary for an experienced health information technician is around $32,000. The hourly wage is about $14. Health information technicians work in an office environment and usually have a standard workweek with no evening or weekend hours. The growing demand for workers in this field means that there may be increased opportunities to advance into a supervisory or training role.

Medical Assistant

Medical assistants are the people who keep medical offices and hospital floors running smoothly. They are in charge of the administrative and clerical end of things and also help with some clinical work. They check patients in and out, schedule appointments, update and file charts, and handle a lot of paperwork/computer work, such as sending specimens to the lab and forwarding information to the medical billing and coding staff. They also sometimes perform some basic clinical functions, such as taking blood pressure.

About 60 percent of all medical assistants work in doctors' offices. Others work in hospitals, clinics, or outpatient settings; some work for other health care providers such as optometrists. Wherever you work can be a good starting point to get a feel for the different aspects of health care and working with patients. Medical assistants in hospitals usually work on medical floors and are often called unit service assistants or unit clerks. They handle the many administrative and clerical tasks involved with the care of a hospitalized patient. Most medical assistants work a 40-hour, Monday to Friday week; some employers, especially hospitals, may require occasional evening and weekend work.

Many medical assistants learn their skills on the job; a background in administrative and clerical work is helpful. Employers often prefer to hire medical assistants who have completed a one- to two-year training program at a community college or vocational school. The courses teach skills such as basic medical terminology, office management, medical recordkeeping, and insurance processing. Most one-year courses offer a certificate; most two-year courses offer an associate's degree.

Within an office or hospital setting, medical assistants do not have much opportunity for advancement. To get ahead, they often move on to other areas of medical administration, such as health information or the coding and billing departments. Because a medical assistant assists with many aspects of health care, this is a good background for moving into patient care areas such as becoming an LPN or cardiac technician.

Certification is not required to become a medical assistant, but many employers prefer it. At least four agencies offer general certification. Several others offer specialized certification, such as certification as a podiatric assistant. A good starting point for looking into certification is the American Association of Medical Assistants, which offers the general Certified Medical Assistant (CMA) certification.

The Bureau of Labor Statistics ranks medical assisting as one of the fastest-growing occupations in health care. In 2009 about 417,000 people were working as medical assistants, and demand is expected to grow by 148,000 workers by 2016—an increase of a whopping 35 percent.

Salaries for medical assistants average around $27,000; on an hourly basis, the average wage is around $15.

Medical Coder

Every time a patient goes to the doctor, has a test done, or receives any other medical service, someone—usually an insurance company or Medicaid or Medicare—gets a bill. A code number called the current procedural terminology (CPT) on the bill tells the insurer who the patient is, what the diagnosis is, and what was done. Keeping track of all those codes and billing for them is a fulltime job for a medical coder, because there are more than 9,000 CPTs that cover every type of health care service provided by a health care practitioner or facility. On top of that, there are more than 13,500 code numbers for diagnoses. These are called ICD-9 codes for the huge book that lists them all, the *International Classification of Diseases*, ninth edition.

Medical coders sort through patient charts to assign the right codes and make sure the bill is sent out promptly so that health care providers are reimbursed correctly for their services. Accurate coding is crucial to keeping the health care system running smoothly. Inaccurate or incomplete coding or billing leads to payment delays or sometimes no payment at all, along with a lot of complaints from patients.

Medical coders often learn their skills on the job, but today the field is more complex and people who have completed a training course are preferred. Short courses, usually no longer than six months, are offered at community colleges, technical schools, and through distance learning. Medical coders can take a certification exam offered by the American Academy of Professional Coders. Passing the exam lets you use the credential Certified Professional Coder (CPC). This is a good area for medical assistants to consider— their background in medical terminology and patient care can be a big help in picking up the skills.

The medical billing and coding field is growing fast, and changes that increase access to the health care system will lead to even more rapid growth. Salaries for experienced workers in this area range between $36,000 and $44,500. About two of every five medical coders and billers work in hospitals. The rest work in doctors' offices, nursing homes, outpatient care centers, and home health care agencies.

Medical Transcriptionist

A medical transcriptionist is an expert in the language of medicine. Medical transcriptionists listen to recordings made by doctors and other health care professionals and transcribe them into medical reports, letters, and other administrative documents. Today medical transcriptionists mostly work with digital recordings, often sent over the Internet from a separate location; voice recognition technology is increasingly important. To transcribe the files or check a document produced using voice recognition, medical transcriptionists need a very thorough knowledge of medical terminology and medical jargon, good grammar and spelling ability, and good computer skills.

Transcriptionists often work in office areas of hospitals, outpatient care centers, and ambulatory surgery centers. Many transcriptionists work from home. Because medical terminology is so complex, medical transcriptionists usually get into the field by taking a training course at a community college, technical school, or online. If possible, choose a course accredited by the Approval Committee for Certificate Programs (AACP) of the Association for Healthcare Documentation Integrity (AHDI). Certificate courses usually take about a year; associate's degree courses usually take two years. The AHDI offers two exam-based certifications: the basic credential, Registered Medical Transcriptionist (RMT) and the more advanced credential Certified Medical Transcriptionist (CMT). Many employers prefer to hire workers who have AHDI certification.

Job growth for medical transcriptionists will be moderate in the future. In 2006 about 98,000 people worked as medical transcriptionists. The Bureau of Labor Statistics estimates that by 2016 about 112,000 transcriptionists will be needed, an increase of about 13,000 workers. Salaries in this area are generally in the range of $23,000 to $36,000.

Chapter 4

Tips for Success

Whether you are starting your first job in health care or moving onward and upward to a new position, your career path will go more smoothly if you remember that professionalism is always your top concern. What does that mean? Your patients must always come first—their care and safety is your top priority. The best way you can help your patients is by being as well-trained, responsible, respectful, and caring as possible.

Health care is not always an easy profession. The physical work of being on your feet all day helping patients is tiring. The emotional work of being sympathetic yet keeping a degree of professional detachment can be very demanding, especially for people who work with very sick patients. The level of responsibility is high—your patients depend on you. And as in any other workplace, there are conflicts with bosses and coworkers.

Burning out is a common problem for health care workers. The long hours, shift work, stress, and sometimes low pay make them leave health care for some other type of work. In fact, about one in five new nurses leave the profession within a few years of graduating, even though they have worked very hard to earn their degrees.

In this chapter you will find the information you need to move ahead with your career successfully and avoid the stress and burnout that come with health care work.

Being Professional

As a brand-new health care worker, you may not feel very professional, despite your training. That first job, with all the responsibilities for patients, can be challenging. Being professional is more a matter of attitude than experience, however. If you are consistently courteous and respectful to both your patients and your fellow workers, you are off to a good start. As you continue on in your health care career, those values will help you move ahead into positions of more responsibility.

The modern American health care system is confusing even to people who have been working in it a long time. The system is very hierarchical: Orders tend to come from the top (the doctors) down in a strict sequence—and what each type of health care worker can

Problem
Solving

Coping with Difficult Patients

Your patients all deserve to be treated with dignity and courtesy, even when they are not cooperative. The same goes for the patient's family. The fear, anxiety, pain, confusion, and anger that go with serious health problems can make people say nasty things to you, the health care worker doing your best to help them. Try to remain calm and listen even when you are being verbally attacked. After all, underneath the shouting there might be a real issue that needs to handled. If you cannot calm the patient or family member down, bring in your supervisor before the situation gets any worse. Sometimes patients and family members behave in racist ways. Some patients may refuse to be treated by someone who is African American, Hispanic, or a member of another minority. Sometimes a female patient will object to care from a male nurse or patient care aide. These are difficult situations to handle. Family members will often intervene and help the patient accept the care. If no family member is present, and if the patient is capable of understanding you, tell him or her firmly that you are the assigned caregiver and that you will do your best to help. Do not argue or get defensive, and bring in your supervisor immediately if you cannot resolve the issue on the spot.

do is very strictly regulated by state and federal law. As a health care worker, you need to have a very good understanding of your scope of practice, or exactly what you can and cannot do with patients and clients. Most of that will be clearly spelled out to you during your training and as part of your licensing or certification. If you have any doubts about doing something for or to a patient, always check first with your supervisor. And if your supervisor asks you to do something that you think you are not qualified to do or that is outside your scope of practice, raise the issue immediately (emergencies excepted).

At the top of the health care hierarchy are the doctors, who have the highest level of training and responsibility for diagnosing and treating medical problems. In most cases, it is a doctor who sees the patient, decides what the problem is, orders tests such as blood work and CT scans, prescribes medications, performs procedures such as colonoscopies, and decides if a patient needs to be in the hospital. Doctors also refer patients to specialists and for treatments such as physical therapy. Because doctors are so highly trained and because they are usually also extremely busy, they rely heavily on their office staff members, including nurse practitioners, physician assistants, and registered nurses, to do a lot of the less specialized work.

Next below the doctors in the medical hierarchy are highly trained professionals such as nurse practitioners and physician assistants. These people can do many of the same things as a doctor, including prescribing drugs in some states. In practice, they deal with less serious health issues and simple procedures, such as routine checkups and minor illnesses, leaving the doctors more time to deal with serious problems and more complex cases.

Registered nurses are next on the medical hierarchy. In hospitals, doctors' offices, clinics, and everywhere else, nurses are the backbone of health care. They carry out the orders a doctor gives for a patient and supervise staffers such as LPNs and CNAs. The old stereotype, where a male doctor barks orders at a female nurse, who meekly replies, "Yes, doctor," no longer applies (although some doctors still think it does). In modern medicine nurses are not just order-takers—they are active caregivers and patient advocates as part of a collaborative system. They work with doctors, not for them, and they always put their patients first. The same applies for therapists of various sorts. A doctor must refer a patient to a physical therapist for treatment, but the therapist decides the best approach to the treatment and how to administer it. When in doubt or if there is a

Everyone

Knows

Uniforms and Footwear

Health care workers with patient contact, such as nurses, LPNs, dental hygienists, and so on, are usually required to wear uniforms at work. In many cases, that means scrubs—a short-sleeved, collarless pullover shirt and trousers. Scrubs are designed to be simple—there is no ornamentation or cuffs that can carry germs—easy to get into, easy to wash, and inexpensive. Uniforms help set the staff members apart from everyone else in the hospital. Different departments or different types of workers may have different colored scrubs or uniforms. If you are required to wear a uniform, your employer will probably give you an allowance to buy them. Do not forget your nametag—it is considered a part of your uniform.

Health care workers are on their feet all day, so comfortable shoes are a must. Check with your employer before you buy any shoes, however. Some employers do not allow open-back clogs, Crocs, or sandals. Your shoes will probably need have at least a strap back and closed toes—this helps prevent trips, falls, sticks with dropped sharps, and contamination with spilled fluids. They may need to be white or a color that matches your uniform.

A professional appearance also means very light makeup (if any), no perfume, trimmed nails, neatly trimmed facial hair for men, and very little jewelry. An analog watch with a second hand is a must, and wedding bands are fine, but any other jewelry gets in the way and carries germs—and rings have been known to end up in the trash when stripping off latex gloves.

problem, the therapist consults with the doctor to decide the best treatment.

Just as nurses work with doctors to provide patient care, health care workers such as patient aides and LPNs work with nurses to make sure patients are getting good care. Although there is a clear hierarchy of training and responsibility, everyone needs to work together. For example, patient care aides, because they work closely with their patient, can often spot problems that need to be reported to the nurse.

Medical Etiquette

Things will sometimes go wrong in your work. Miscommunication in health care is common. Charts, equipment, and sometimes even patients get misplaced. Things that should have been done are forgotten, fellow workers come in late, mistakes are made—and tensions rise. Displeasure at mistakes and problems tends to get sent down the line from the top. If you are the one being criticized, or if you have to criticize someone else, follow medical etiquette. Reprimands should be given in private, one–on-one—and never, ever in front of patients. Unfortunately, in medicine this etiquette does not get followed as often as it should. At some point in your career you are going to get yelled at, probably in front of other people, whether

Everyone
Knows

Coping with Shift Work

A drawback to health care work is that you may have to do shift work, including nightshifts. Most nonhospital shifts are three weeks long and rotate through morning/afternoon, afternoon/evening, and nights (if necessary). In many hospitals, nursing and patient care aide shifts are 12 hours straight for three or four days in a row; you usually alternate a few weeks of days with a few weeks of nights. Shift work can make it hard to synch your schedule with your family and friends. It is also hard on your body and is a major cause of worker burnout in health care. If you are working nights, you might have trouble sleeping enough during the day. The transition from one shift to the other can also disrupt your sleep patterns. Shift work insomnia is a big problem. You can cope by asking people not to call you during the day when you need to be sleeping and to be quiet around the house—no loud TV or vacuuming while you are getting your shuteye. You will sleep better in the day if your bedroom has heavy curtains to block out light; some people find sleep masks are helpful. To block out daytime noise, try using a white noise machine, fan, air conditioner, or some other device, or use earplugs. Some people find that prescription sleeping pills help you adjust when you move from nights to days or vice versa.

or not you deserve it. If you truly made a mistake, apologize, do what you must to fix your error, learn from the experience, and move on. If you truly did nothing wrong, or if you are being blamed for someone else's mistake, try to respond tactfully, without being defensive. And again, learn from the experience and move on.

Sometimes when things go wrong in health care, it is because someone has made a medical mistake that did or could harm a patient. There are plenty of ways for even very experienced people to make mistakes. Fortunately, most medical errors are not serious and do not cause any harm—being twenty minutes late with a patient's medication, for instance, is common on a busy hospital floor. Of course, if the patient is waiting for pain medicine, that twenty minutes can seem like a very long time. More serious medication errors would be giving the patient the wrong medication or the wrong dose. Other common medical errors include needle sticks, not recording information in the patient's chart or recording it incorrectly, or failing to use sterile techniques when doing a procedure. The most common error of all? Failing to wash your hands or use a sanitizing gel before touching a patient.

If you see a medical mistake about to happen—a drug is about to be given to the wrong patient, for instance, or proper sterile technique is not being used—speak up. It does not matter who is about to make the error, even if it is a senior doctor. You owe it to the patient and to yourself to make sure the mistake does not happen if you can prevent it. If you are uncertain about how to do something or have a question about it, ask for help. It is better to appear a little uncertain to a coworker or your supervisor than to make a medical error that could harm your patient. And if you do make a mistake, report it to your supervisor at once. Delay, denial, or trying to cover up the error could be grounds for firing you.

Sometimes medical mistakes are not obvious or do not happen in front of other workers. If you think a fellow worker has erred, it is your duty to report it. You can probably do this anonymously if you prefer to avoid confrontation.

Planning Your Career

When you start your career in health care, you are putting your feet on the first rung of a career ladder that can take you as far as you are willing and able to go. In a 2006 study of health care workers in northwest Tennessee, here are some of the career ladders climbed by workers at one hospital:

Home health care aide ⟶ certified nursing assistant ⟶ LPN ⟶ registered nurse

Receptionist ⟶ medical secretary ⟶ medical records ⟶ billing and coding clerk

Certified nursing assistant ⟶ lab assistant ⟶ phlebotomist ⟶ lab technician

Nurses' aide ⟶ LPN ⟶ RN ⟶ clinical nurse specialist

EMT ⟶ paramedic ⟶ respiratory therapy technician ⟶ respiratory therapist

In health care, it is possible to start anywhere and move ahead with proper training and education. Is it easy? Definitely not. It is hard to work and also go to school, and it is sometimes hard to find ways to pay for your training. But is it worthwhile? Definitely. Every step up the career ladder means more pay, more responsibility, and more chances for further training and advancement.

Choosing the Best Training for You

Training and education are the best investments you can make in your career, even if you have been working in health care for years. Your skills are in demand, and the better your skills are, and the more training you have, the more job options you will have.

Health care training programs are generally found at the college and community college level, through vocational and technical schools, and through employers. Which program is best for you will depend on many factors, including location, the type of degree you want, the area you want to specialize in, and how you will pay for your education.

⟶ Location. When looking for the right program for you, look close to home first. Chances are you live near a community college that is part of your state's higher education system. You might also live near a state or private college or university. It is also possible that you live near an accredited vocational or technical school. If you are planning to work while going to school, a program nearby is the most logical choice.

➡ Degrees. Before deciding on a program, look at what sort of degree you will earn. A four-year bachelor's degree or a two-year associate's degree will give you the most value for your tuition, but you do not necessarily need to start out with these degrees. The whole question of degrees, licenses, and certifications is very complex and will be discussed in more detail later in this chapter.

➡ Specialties. You can probably find a nearby training program to become an LPN or registered nurse, an EMT, and many other patient care professions. For more specialized areas, such as becoming a diagnostic medical sonographer, you may have to look for programs outside your region. Whatever program you choose, be sure it is fully accredited, as will be explained below.

Education in health care can be expensive, but there are also ways to keep the costs down and to get some financial help. Look into postgraduate vocational programs through your local school system that will train you for some health care positions, such as being a certified nursing assistant or pharmacy tech. Going to a community college or state university is one of the best bargains in health care education. As a resident of your state your tuition is much lower than it would be at a private college. You may be eligible for state tuition assistance if you attend a state school or if you attend a private college or a vocational or technical school in your state. A wide range of scholarships and state and federal loan programs is also available to you—too many to discuss here. Check with your school's financial aid office. Help is available even if you are going to school only part-time or if you need to do some make-up work before you can begin your training program.

Because minorities are seriously underrepresented in every area of health care, there are many programs at the local and state level designed to recruit them into training programs. The programs usually offer substantial financial aid and a lot of academic and social support to help you succeed. If you qualify, these programs can be very helpful for overcoming educational and financial barriers to your training.

Another way to cover at least some of the costs for your education is through your employer. Larger employers, especially large hospitals, often have tuition reimbursement plans that will pay for some or even all of your courses as long as you work there. Large employers such as big hospitals also often have in-house programs that train workers to move up the career ladder. Someone who cleans patients' rooms in the hospital can take classes through the employer to become a nursing aide. And with that credential, the next step up is to become a certified nursing assistant or LPN, using tuition reimbursement from the employer to help pay for the training. At some large employers, formal degree programs are in place to help you climb the career ladder while you work. These programs are usually geared toward underrepresented minorities and low-income health workers. They let you earn while you learn in a very supportive environment right at the facility. The only problem with these programs is that they are hard to find. Most are offered through major health care employers and are so popular that they do not have to advertise much. To find an in-house training program near you, check with the largest hospital in the area.

Joining the military is also a good way to get into health care—if you qualify, you can be trained in many areas of health care, such as respiratory therapy or surgical technology. Transferring these skills to the civilian world is usually easy to do. You can also look into military nursing scholarship programs that pay for your bachelor's degree; you begin your service only after you graduate and agree to serve for a specified number of years (usually five or six). Nurses who already have their degrees are in great demand by the military. If you decide to enlist as a nurse, you will be commissioned as an officer. You will have excellent opportunities for gaining a lot of experience quickly and for promotion. You will also have opportunities for continuing your training into a specialty area, such as becoming a nurse practitioner. The college benefits that are available to anyone who serves in the armed forces are a great way to pay for your health care training once you return to civilian life.

What about online degrees? These are less expensive and more flexible than attending classes, especially if you are already working and have to cope with shift work and family life. In some cases, these programs may be right for you. Many programs now let you do at least some of the work through distance learning. But because training in health care also involves hands-on clinical work with real patients, you will not be able to do all your degree or certificate online. (The exception would be training for clerical jobs such as coding clerk.) Look for distance learning options from accredited institutions—do not give your money to an online school unless you have checked it out carefully and know that your credential will be accepted by employers and state authorities.

Choose the Best Program

Education is a serious matter in health care. To a large extent—perhaps more than it should—where you get your degree or training counts. When selecting a program, aim high. Go for the best school you can get into. What makes it the best? All the usual things: accreditation, good opportunities for clinical training, small class size, and a reputation for excellence. The better your school's reputation, the better your résumé will look to a potential employer or

Best
Practice

Hand Sanitation

One of the very first things you learned in your training was hand sanitation. You were taught when and how to wash your hands, when and how to use a sanitizing gel, and when to wear gloves. Your instructors emphasized how important this is to avoid spreading infections. And when you were tested on practical and clinical skills, if you did not automatically wash your hands and put on gloves if needed, you automatically failed—even if hand sanitation was not on the list of items being tested. Even so, lack of proper hand sanitation is still a problem in health care. The most common failure is not washing for long enough. Here is the rule to remember: Wash with soap under running water for 20 seconds—just long enough to sing all of the "Twinkle, twinkle, little star" song (to yourself). Gloves are required for any procedure that is invasive, such as inserting an IV or removing stitches. Some people are allergic to the latex used in disposable gloves. To solve this fairly common problem, most gloves today are latex-free. If you are allergic, though, do not assume—check the package to be sure the gloves have no latex.

when you are putting in for a promotion. You can find out about class size and so on from the school, but reputation is a little harder to assess. Programs that are affiliated with large medical centers are often felt to offer the best training and faculty. Programs that are longer or more demanding also have higher reputations. Ask the recruiter or admissions officer about recent graduates. How many of them found jobs in the field within three to six months? Who are the employers? What are the salaries? You want to know that most graduates have quickly found good jobs with good employers.

Preceptors and Mentors

Your first job after graduation is a stressful time, even if you have work experience in other fields. Instead of being responsible for only a few patients under careful supervision, now you are in charge of six to ten patients—on your own. To help you succeed in your new job, you will probably be assigned a preceptor or mentor for at least your first three to six months. A preceptor (the word comes from the Latin word meaning tutor) is an experienced professional, such as a senior nurse, who is formally assigned to help you learn the ins and outs of your new position, to answer your questions, and to advise and encourage you through a stressful time. First-year nurses and other professionals, such as physical therapists, are almost always assigned a preceptor. Once you are more experienced, you will not need a preceptor as you move up or as you start a new job. Mentors are a less formal way of helping new workers learn and adjust. Your mentor will probably be someone you work with regularly. He or she will be there to help you handle new situations and answer questions. As you gain experience in your career, becoming a mentor or preceptor yourself is a great way to give back. In some cases, formal mentoring or being a preceptor carries some extra pay and may count toward your continuing education requirements.

Degreed, Certified, Registered, Licensed

Today almost every health care job requires some sort of degree, certification, registration, or licensing. The terminology can be a little confusing, especially because different states may have different names and different requirements for what is basically the same job. For example, a licensed practical nurse (LPN) is someone with at least one year of training in basic patient care such as bathing, taking vital signs, and changing bandages and who has also passed a licensing test given by the state where he or she works. (In most states, the licensing test is the national NCLEX-PN.) In California and Texas, however, these workers are called licensed vocational nurses (LVN). They do exactly the same work, but in these states extensive practical experience (at least 51 months of direct patient care in a hospital setting) can substitute for formal training and passing a test.

Bearing in mind that terminology and requirements vary, let us take a closer look at what credentials you need to start and advance your health care career.

Degrees

Many health care training programs offered through community colleges and colleges and universities offer an academic degree. If you complete a two-year program, you will probably receive an associate's degree (some programs offer a certificate instead of a degree). If you complete a four-year program, you will receive a bachelor's degree. If you go on to advanced study, you can get a master's degree or even a doctorate (Ph.D.) degree. Many health care workers start with an associate's degree and study part time to earn higher degrees. In some cases, your employer will help you with tuition. The extra work of going to school part-time pays off down the road. More education usually means higher pay and better career opportunities.

Academic degrees are a great credential in health care, but they are not needed for every job. Some jobs in health care, such as home health aide, require only a high school diploma or GED and may even be open to people without these degrees. Other good jobs in health care, such certified nursing assistant or licensed practical nurse, require short training courses, usually a year or less.

Some shorter training programs (usually shorter than one year) offer a certificate showing that you have completed the course satisfactorily. A certificate is not a degree, and it is not the same as certification (see below), but it is a credential you worked to earn and it shows you have training and commitment to your area. Certificates make you stand out among other job candidates. If you decide to go on for a degree program, a certificate may help strengthen your application.

Certification

The essential first step toward a solid career as a health care practitioner is certification from an accredited professional governing body. Certification means you have graduated from an accredited training program and have met a high national professional standard. Even in states or for jobs where certification is not required, many employers prefer to hire people who have the credential. Certification proves you have the education, skills, and commitment to do the job. If you are a radiation technologist, for instance, the American Registry of Radiologic Technologists (ARRT) authorizes your certification. You can be certified as an RT only if you meet the educational and ethical standards of the ARRT—and pass its tough certification exam.

The education requirement for certification almost always means completion of a training program offered by an accredited institution.

Everyone
Knows

Choose an Accredited Program

The high demand for health care professionals has led to some big problems with unaccredited training programs. These fraudulent programs exploit people who want to get into health care, especially in jobs such as home health care aide or certified nursing assistant. They take your money and provide some training, but because they are not accredited, you will not meet the education requirement for certification. On top of that, the education you get probably will not prepare you well for the certification exam. In fact, if the school is not properly certified, you may not even be allowed to take the exam.

If you are considering a career in health care, avoid a costly mistake. Be sure the training program you select is accredited by the Committee on Accreditation for Allied Health Education Programs (CAAHEP) or by a national professional organization—preferably both. When in doubt, do not take the word of the recruiter—check with whatever state agency regulates your professional area to be sure your training program is acceptable. State agencies often have a blacklist of programs that do not meet state standards.

For many health care professions, that means a program that meets the tough standards set by the Committee on Accreditation for Allied Health Education Programs (CAAHEP). For other professions, the training program must be accredited by an organization that is usually related to the main professional organization in the field. Many approved training programs offer an associate's or bachelor's degree upon graduation. Accredited training programs in areas that do not require degrees, such as licensed practical nursing, prepare you for the national certification exam.

If you attend a U.S. training program that is *not* accredited by CAAHEP or some other recognized accrediting agency, there is a very good chance that you will *not* be allowed to take the certification exam in your area. Before you enroll in any health care training program, make sure it is accredited!

The ethical requirements for certification usually mean that you have a good moral character, have not been convicted of a serious crime, and agree to abide by the ethical standards of the governing body for your area of health care. Letters of reference from instructors or employers may be required.

Passing the certification exam for your specialty can be challenging. These exams are designed to test both your classroom knowledge and your clinical training. Some exams include both a written test and a practical test to demonstrate your skills. The practical exam to become a certified nursing assistant (CNA), for instance, requires you to demonstrate a number of basic skills, such as helping a patient move safely from the bed to a chair.

Once you have gotten your basic certification in an area of health care such as speech-language pathology, it is time to move on to additional certification in a specialty. As health care gets more complicated and uses more and more advanced technology, certification programs in specialty areas have expanded. For instance, licensed practical nurses can apply for certification in the special skills needed for working in nursing homes and other facilities that provide long-term care.

Additional certification means more studying and additional costs for study materials and exam fees. Depending on your practice area and your employer, you may get time off to study and you may get some expense reimbursement. More important, additional certification is a smart career move. It proves you have a high level of competence in your area. When employers have to choose among several candidates for a job, the one with the best credentials is most likely to stand out. More certifications can also lead to better pay. According to the American Nursing Association, registered nurses with specialty certifications earn between $8,000 and $10,000 more a year than those without certification.

For many areas of health care, the credentialing agency is a nonprofit corporation that is an offshoot of one or more professional societies. For example, the American Nurses Credentialing Center is the credentialing arm of the American Nurses Association. In some areas of health care, more than one credentialing organization offers certification. If you are cardiac technologist, for instance, you could be certified by either the Cardiovascular Credentialing International (CCI) or the American Registry of Diagnostic Medical Sonographers (ARDMS). The CCI offers four certifications: Certified Cardiographic Technician (CCT), Registered Cardiac Sonographer (RCS), Registered Vascular Specialist (RVS), and Registered Cardiovascular Invasive Specialist (RCIS). The ARDMS offers Registered Diagnostic Cardiac Sonographer (RDCS) and Registered Vascular Technologist (RVT) credentials. There is no significant difference between the two organizations and the requirements for the various specialty certifications. Which one should you choose? Some state licensing boards and some employers may have a preference for one credentialing organization over another. The information is usually available on the state Web sites and in job descriptions. If you are still in school, your academic advisor can help you sort out the best approach, depending in part on where you are studying and where you hope to work after graduation.

Licensing

Today, with the increasing professionalization of health care, some sort of certification is needed for most jobs. When a state also requires a license to practice in a particular area such as respiratory therapy, certification is almost a necessity. In fact, for many health care professionals such as occupational therapists, the national certification exam from a credentialing organization doubles as the state licensing exam.

Because the need for a license, and the requirements to get it, vary among the different states, there are some licensed jobs that do not necessarily require additional certification. However, these jobs are scarce and getting scarcer all the time. One big reason is that the Centers for Medicaid and Medicare Services have strict requirements for reimbursement. Many services will not be reimbursed if they are performed by an uncertified health care worker. What this means is that more and more health care jobs now require certification. In 2008, for instance, CMS began requiring certification for all kidney dialysis technicians.

Generally speaking, the more responsibility you have for direct patient care, the more likely it is that your state will require you to have a license. Doctors, nurses, practical nurses, physical therapists, respiratory therapists, and many others are usually licensed. The education, examination, and experience requirements for getting the license also vary quite a bit. And just to make life more complicated for health care workers, the state agency that is in charge of licensing also goes by a variety of names. In New York state, for instance, the Office of the Professions is in charge of health care licensing. Although New York has a state department of health, the Office of the Professions is actually part of the state department of education. When in doubt, check with the state to find the right department. The information is often on the state Web site; many professional organizations also can help you track down the right department within a particular state.

State Designation

In some areas of health care, especially nursing, your credentials can go beyond basic licensure. In many states, nurses and some other health care professionals, such as respiratory therapists, can take advanced classes that lead to a specialty credential such as nurse practitioner or advanced practice nurse. Having a state designation lets you practice at a more advanced level—but only in that state. Because state requirements for advanced certification vary very widely, your state designation may not be accepted in another state.

Registration

Once a certificate or license is granted, it is usually good for life within that state—as long as you maintain your registration. This means your name is listed on the state registry of qualified professionals in your field. Regulations vary, but you will almost certainly have to reregister on a regular basis, usually once every few years. At that time you may have to show that you have done the required number of hours of continuing education. You may also have to show you have taken any programs that the state has started requiring since your last registration, such as a child abuse recognition class. There is usually a fee for renewing your registration.

If you temporarily stop working in your licensed field, you can usually request inactive status and skip the re-registration requirement until you are ready to go back. Check with your state licensing agency for details. Be sure to get a clear idea of what you will need to do to reregister after a few years or more away. You may have to make up all the required courses since you suspended your registration. Today the demand for registered health care workers is so high that hospitals and colleges run refresher courses for people who have let their registration lapse and want to return to work.

National Certification

In addition to state certification and licensure, some areas of health care also offer national certification, also called board certification. These credentials are awarded by a nationally recognized certifying body, such as the American Academy of Nurse Practitioners Certifying Board. To be certified, you usually have to meet high educational standards, pass a tough exam, and have extensive work experience in your specialty. If you meet all the requirements, you can add the appropriate letters after your name. In the case of a board-certified nurse practitioner, for instance, that would be NP-C, the C indicating certified.

Continuing Education

Just about every job in health care has a continuing education (CE) requirement (sometimes also called continuing competency). It is mandated by the state where you work and is almost always a requirement for getting your license or certification renewed. It may even be a requirement for keeping your job. In many states, for example, health care professionals are required to take certain courses, such as infection control and recognizing child abuse. You may need to update the requirement on a regular basis, usually once every few years. Similarly, you may need to be recertified in some skills, such as CPR, on a regular basis.

How many hours of continuing education you have to do each year will depend a lot on your job title, your professional qualifications, and what your state demands. What counts as continuing education will also vary quite a bit, again depending on what you do and where you do it. If you hold a state license or certification, you can generally expect to need anywhere from 10 to 30 hours of continuing education each year. If you are not sure how many hours of CE you need or what type of CE is acceptable, check with your human resources department or with the state agency that regulates your area of health care. Do not wait until you are up against the deadline to find out what you need to do! Failure to complete continuing education and mandated education on a timely basis could be grounds for losing your license.

You have a lot of options for meeting your CE requirement, including:

- Formal continuing education courses, workshops, and seminars approved by the governing agency for your area of health care
- Formal academic study in courses credited toward a degree from an accredited program
- Self study, using materials provided by an approved sponsor (distance learning is often acceptable for at least some of your mandated CE hours)
- Independent study
- Tests through print and online journals
- Mentoring another professional on a one-to-one basis
- Publishing an article in a peer-reviewed journal or writing or editing a chapter in a book
- Making a presentation or speech at a professional conference
- Teaching an in-service training program

Formal courses and formal academic study are the simplest ways to complete your annual CE requirements. If you take credit-bearing courses you are getting a double benefit: you fulfill your requirement while working toward your advanced degree. Remember that clock hours are not the same as CE hours. A 10-hour course may not count as 10 hours of CE. Similarly, in most cases it takes several independent or self-study clock hours to make up one CE hour. In many cases, you can do only a portion (usually up to half) of the required hours with self-study or online work; the rest may have to be done in person in classes and seminars or in some other way.

Many, many CE courses are available in a variety of formats. You could attend a CE seminar at a professional conference, for

INTERVIEW

Twenty-Five Years on the Job

Chuck Curlee, RRT, CRTT
Respiratory therapist, Los Angeles, California

Why did you decide to go into respiratory therapy?

I became a respiratory therapist more than 25 years ago. I had two bachelor's degrees, one in psychology and one in industrial management, but the jobs I had bored me—I did not feel I was making a difference to anyone. I started looking around for a new field I could enter relatively quickly. Health care interested me, and I had a friend who was a respiratory therapist. He told me all about it, both the pros and the cons, and soon I was enrolled in a two-year program at a nearby community college.

One of the questions I was asked at the admissions interview was, "How would you resolve a conflict with a nurse?" I said I would try to discuss the issue and that if we could not work it out, I'd ask my supervisor to step in. Another question was, "What would you do if a doctor gave you an order that you knew would harm the patient?" I said I would refuse, that doctors are not infallible and my first responsibility is to the patient. Those turned out to be the right answers not just for the interview, but for what really happens on the job.

Where are you working now?

I am now a staff respiratory therapist at a large level 2 trauma hospital in Los Angeles. I spend 90 percent of my time in the adult intensive

instance. Depending on the length of the seminar, you could earn one to three hours of CE time. You could also take a CE course offered through your employer (often sponsored by a drug or medical device maker) or at a local community college. In-service courses, where you get time off from work to attend training sessions (to learn how to use a new piece of equipment, for instance), may count toward CE.

Online courses are increasingly popular as a way to meet some of your CE requirements. (Any requirement where you have to demonstrate a hands-on skill, such as using medical equipment, probably cannot be met through an online course.) Today, these courses are usually just as acceptable as attending a class in person. One care unit, mostly treating trauma victims. Some have been in car crashes, but because of the neighborhood the hospital serves, I also see a lot of shooting and stabbing victims. My patients may not always be model citizens, but they still deserve good medical treatment. During my shift, I am usually responsible for three to four patients. When a patient is unstable, I may spend an hour or more constantly adjusting the ventilator to keep him alive.

How do you handle the shift work and overtime?

As a new RT, I was assigned to the nightshift at my first job. Most people do not like that shift, but I was always a night person and it worked out well for me. In fact, I have been working mostly night shifts ever since. RTs, like a lot of allied health workers, usually work 12-hour shifts. Over a two-week pay period, I work four 12-hour days one week and three 12-hour days the next week. In addition, I usually put in between 36 and 40 hours of overtime in that two-week period, so on average I work about 60 hours a week. In the course of a shift, I get half an hour for lunch and a 15-minute break for every four hours I work. That is only an hour and 15 minutes off during a 12-hour shift. The job can be very stressful and the long hours are tiring. I sometimes get into my car, drive home, and fall asleep in the driveway.

What's your advice to people getting started in the field?

For new RTs or RTs starting a new job, I recommend being adaptable. Do not take the attitude that you know everything already. Especially when you are not sure what to do, listen to the people with more experience.

popular free online approach is reading an article in a professional journal online and then taking a short online quiz about it. Each quiz you pass gives you a small amount of credit—often just half an hour—toward your CE requirement.

There are so many available courses that choosing one that is right for you can be confusing. Here is how to pick a CE program that is worthwhile and appropriate for you:

➜ The provider is reputable and established. Look for courses offered through professional organizations, at colleges, or at a professional conference. Avoid commercial companies that do not have established track records.

➡ The provider is accredited by a reputable professional organization. If you take a course through an unaccredited organization, it is possible your work will not be accepted toward your CE requirement. Read the course offering carefully to be sure—and when in doubt, check with the state agency for your professional area.

➡ Be sure the course is appropriate for you. Does the topic relate directly to your work? Will you be able to apply what you learn? Will the information be presented at the right level for you? Read the course description carefully, especially the program objectives. Contact the provider for more information if you need it.

➡ Watch out for bias. Many CE courses are sponsored by drug manufacturers, medical device makers, and other

Everyone
Knows

Foreign Training

Health care workers who receive their training in another country can be certified or licensed in the United States. The requirements vary from state to state and from job title to job title. An important aspect of getting American credentials is having your education verified by an official agency. Foreign-trained nurses and licensed practical nurses, for example, must have their credentials verified by the Commission on Graduates of Foreign Nursing Schools (CGFNS). Once the credentials are verified, they are then considered and evaluated by the state licensing authority to see if they meet the state's requirements. Because the requirements are often very strict, foreign graduates usually have to pass the same certification and licensing exams as people trained in the United States. Most states also require foreign graduates to pass the Test of English as a Foreign Language (TOEFL).

Visa requirements for noncitizens to work legally in the United States are far too complex to discuss here. In most cases, noncitizens are recruited in their home country, usually through their school or an agency. The visa paperwork is done by the U.S. employer before they arrive.

corporations. The good part is that the course may be free or inexpensive and will meet your CE requirements. The problem is that the information may be biased in favor of the company's products. The phrase "sponsored by an unrestricted educational grant" from a company name tells you the course has a corporate sponsor. Also look for financial disclosure information from the speaker or instructor—often they have a financial tie to the company whose products they are discussing.

➡ Double-check that your course hours will count toward your CE, licensure, or certification requirements. Some courses may just not be acceptable at all. You may also face some limitations on self-study or online work. Always check with your state agency or accrediting organization.

Some CE offerings, usually the ones sponsored by industry, are free. As long as they are offered by an accredited provider and you are comfortable with any biases that may be built in to the course, that is fine. When courses have fees, the amounts can vary quite a bit, depending on how the course is taught (online, self-study materials, in person) and who is providing it. Sometimes CE fees are included in the registration fee for a conference.

All those education hours can add up to real cost. Your employer may offer in-service courses or sponsor classes that count toward your CE requirement. Your employer may also have a budget for staff education and can pay some or all of the cost of a course. When you are paying yourself, look for courses that use grant money to keep the costs down. Keep good records of your participation (the costs may be tax-deductible) and follow through to be sure you get the letter or certificate that will show you completed the course.

Finding Your Job in Health Care

The hunt for the right health care job for you often begins while you are still training for your future career. Your academic advisor or career counselor can help you get a good idea of what the local job prospects are. If you are in a health care program at a community college or vocational school, there may be pipeline to employment at a nearby hospital or nursing home, especially if you do any of your clinical training there. That is not a guarantee of a job once you graduate, but local employers who are familiar with your school feel they already know a lot about you and are willing to give you extra consideration in hiring.

Your school's placement office also often has good contacts with other local and regional employers who are eager to hire well trained new workers. Employers will often send a recruiter to the school to interview students who are near graduation. Schools also hold health care job fairs, where numerous employers set up tables to attract and interview potential employees.

Once you have graduated and are in your first job, do not forget your old school. As an alumnus, you may still be entitled to advice and job leads from the career office. Staying in touch with your classmates through the alumni office is also a good way to network and find out about job leads.

If you are already working and want to move onward and maybe upward to a different job, you have a lot options for finding available positions. Large employers, such as hospitals, want to hold on to valued employees and often give them preference for transfers and promotions. Check with the human resources department to see what is available with your current employer. If you are interested in moving to another large employer, check for job listings on the Web site. Many hospitals and other health centers list openings and let you apply online.

Your job search will take place largely online. A number of reliable Web sites are good sources for health care jobs. Most professional organizations, such as American Physical Therapy Association or the many nursing organizations, now have online job listings placed by potential employers. Access to the listings is generally free to members (and often to nonmembers as well). The sites usually also let you register and post a résumé at no charge. Job postings are an excellent way to get a sense of the available positions and to track down jobs that are right for you. Registering your résumé lets employers who need people with your skills seek you out. Today many employers prefer this approach, because it keeps them from being swamped by hundreds of résumés when they post a job. Employees prefer it as well, because potential employers approach them. The job board approach saves a lot of time and effort at both ends. Take advantage of your membership in a professional organization and post your résumé even if you are not actively job hunting. An employer may be looking for someone with exactly your credentials.

Web sites that list jobs in different health care areas are also useful (see the Resources chapter for a list of some reliable sites). These free sites usually allow you to search for jobs by professional area or by geographic area. Most also allow you to register and post a résumé for free.

Job Fairs

Experienced health care workers are in such demand that employers frequently sponsor job fairs, where one or several employers get together and recruit employees. This is a great way to find a job, because you will be able to identify several opportunities at once, submit your résumé, and even have a short interview on the spot with the recruiter.

To find out about health care job fairs in your area, check your local paper, look for notices on employee bulletin boards at your job, check relevant Web sites such as those of major health care employers, and check with your local and state employment offices. Today there are even virtual job fairs online. If you are interested in relocating, these are a great way to apply for jobs without having to travel.

If you are attending a job fair, research in advance the employers who will be there and target the ones that have jobs most appropriate for your skills or who are places you would really like to work. You can usually find a participants' list in the job fair materials or Web site. Work out a brief introduction for yourself that is tailored to the employer, along the lines of: "I am Clara Nightingale. I am working as a pediatric oncology nurse at Major Medical Center and I am interested in moving up to a nurse manager position." Or maybe, "I am Clara Nightingale. I am working as a pediatric oncology nurse at Small Town Hospital and I am interested in bringing my skills to a larger facility." Be enthusiastic and confident (even if you do not really feel that way) and give the recruiter a firm handshake. The interview will probably be very short, so keep it focused on your skills and qualifications and how they relate to available jobs. Do not ask about salaries and benefits at this point. To wrap up, ask what the next steps are in the recruiting process.

Dress professionally (no scrubs if possible), put on a nametag, and bring plenty of copies of your résumé. Try to get there early—this means you talk to recruiters while they are still fresh, and it leaves you time to explore all the booths at the fair. If the line at

INTERVIEW

Growing Up on the Job

Susan Racemi, RN
Nurse, New York, New York

What got you interested in nursing?

When I was in high school I got a summer job in the business department of the small local hospital. I mostly just carried papers around from one part of the hospital to the others, but I got to see what happens and I got to meet a lot of nurses. I liked what they did. At the end of the day, they had really helped people, and all I had done was move paper around. Even though they were sometimes very cynical about nursing, when I said I was interested in becoming a nurse they were encouraging and gave me some good practical advice. The most valuable advice I got was to go straight for my bachelor's, not to stop with a two-year associate's degree. I did my first two years at a local community college and then I transferred to a state nursing school to finish my bachelor's degree. I got a lot of really good clinical experience in my second two years, because the school was connected to a big regional medical center.

What was your first job like?

I was hired right out of school at the medical center where I trained. That made the first year a lot easier, because I already knew the hospital layout and procedures and I knew some of the nurses and doctors. My preceptor was helpful, but she was only interested in my work in the sense of telling me what to do if I asked her. She was not all that helpful about career advice, and she was not very supportive when it came to the emotional issues, like the first time a patient I was responsible for died. She just said, "Listen, this guy was circling the drain for the past three days. He was going to go no matter what you did." That was true, but I wish she had been more understanding of how I felt. She did make me realize that I had to be a grown-up, that nobody in a busy hospital taking care of really sick people has much time to hold the hand of a first-year nurse. They also do not have much patience with mistakes—I got yelled at a lot when I first started, though fortunately nothing I messed up hurt any patients. I started to get the hang of things and felt a lot more confident after about six months, and I did not get yelled at very much after that. And after a year on the job I felt like an old pro.

Where are you working now?
As a floor nurse in the hospital I ended up working with adult cancer patients, mostly caring for patients recovering from surgery or who were in the hospital to treat complications. I used to moonlight as a nurse at an oncology practice once or twice a week, helping with the outpatients getting chemotherapy. When the years of hospital shift work finally got to me, the doctors at the oncology practice offered me a fulltime job where I could work 7:30 a.m. to 4 p.m. five days a week, with weekends off. I took it and I've been there for eight years now; I got made nurse practice manager about two years ago. I enjoyed hospital work and I sort of miss the rapid pace, but this is a much more normal schedule.

What do you think helps new nurses get ahead?
Be a good coworker. Never be late to start your shift, never duck out early or take too long at breaks. If there is a personality problem, work it out or suck it up—do not complain or talk behind someone's back. Bring good skills to the job and be willing to improve and update them. There is always something new to learn in nursing—new equipment, new drugs, new techniques—and if you do not pay attention during the in-service training and study the material afterward, you could get into trouble later on.

When I was a new nurse, I found that I learned a lot from the patient care aides about the practical aspects of bedside care. They knew right away when they needed help with a patient, either back-up from another aide or higher-level help from a nurse, and they did not hesitate to call for it. That taught me to ask for help right away, rather than risk hurting the patient or myself. Never think that because you have an RN that you know more than someone with less education but a lot more experience.

You also have to learn to handle the hours. Long shifts, weekend shifts, mandatory overtime, and the constant switching back and forth from days to nights can really mess up your social life and your family life. Once you have some seniority, you have somewhat more control over your shifts, which makes life easier. If you get solid experience as a floor nurse in a hospital, you can usually move into a job with more normal hours, like working in a doctors' office or a clinic.

one employer is long, move over to one with a shorter line and come back later. Make a note of everyone you talk to. Ask for business cards or write down the contact information—and be sure to follow up with a thank-you note.

Your Health Care Résumé

A good health care résumé is a bit different from the standard résumé someone might use for moving up in an office environment, for example. As a health care professional you need to do much more than simply list your job responsibilities. Instead, you want to emphasize your qualifications, training, skills, and experience, to say nothing of your achievements.

To accomplish that in a one- or two-page résumé, you will need to be focused and concise. When you are planning out your résumé, be sure to include all these elements:

➡ *Caption.* At the top of the page, list your name, address, telephone numbers, email address, and other contact information.

➡ *Objective statement.* Start your résumé with a strong statement about what you want from your job and what you bring to it. Relate the statement directly to the job you are applying for or to your professional interests and areas of expertise. Be specific. If you are a licensed practical nurse experienced with cancer patients, for instance, a statement like "Challenging position in a hospital setting" does not tell the hiring manager what your qualifications are and how they can be used at that hospital. Instead, your objective statement might read: "LPN position in adult oncology unit."

➡ *Qualifications summary.* In just five to ten short bullet points, describe your basic skills and highlight your abilities. Focus your qualifications to match the job you are applying for. This section is an overview of your skills—you will get down to specific examples later in the résumé. If you are a physical therapy assistant, for example, a qualifications summary statement might be "Six years of experience with knee rehabilitation patients." Your résumé will probably be scanned into a database and then searched by keywords such as oncology or perfusion. Be sure to use nouns that relate to your experience and the job you are applying for so that the computer will pick up your skills correctly.

➨ *Education.* Education often goes last in a traditional résumé, but a health care employer needs to know right away if you meet the educational and licensing requirements for the job. Include all degrees and certifications and information about your licensure if you have one.

➨ *Professional experience.* Next comes a heading for professional experience, where you discuss your current or more recent job and work backward to relevant earlier positions. (You do not need to include entry-level jobs from years ago or jobs that are not related to health care.) Be sure to get your job titles and the dates of your employment right. If you have received any honors or awards, add a heading for them. If you have space, you can add information about related volunteer work, such as being a volunteer EMT or Red Cross instructor. Leave out irrelevant personal information, such as your hobbies or marital status.

Throughout your résumé, emphasize your skills and experience, the types of patients you have worked with, and the settings (ICU, ambulatory surgery center) where you have worked. Include nouns that are specific to your work, such as *infusion, geriatrics,* or *discharge plan.* Also use lots of action verbs. The employment database will look for words related to a specific job but also for words such as *achieve, collaborate, administer, coordinate, prepare, record, improve, prescribe,* and so on. Instead of saying you are "responsible for patient care on a maternity floor," for instance, say you "provide or coordinate patient care for post-delivery patients." Look for verbs that emphasize your ability to take charge and lead in your job, such as *solve, spearhead, manage,* and *supervise.*

Keep your résumé clear and simple, and have someone else check it over for typos and grammatical errors. Save your résumé as a Word file and also as a PDF file; this makes it easier to attach it to e-mails. Also save a version with simple formatting that can be pasted into the body of an e-mail without getting jumbled.

A résumé should always be sent with a cover letter, even if you are sending it by e-mail. Whenever possible, address the cover letter to someone specific—and be sure you have that person's name and title right. A good cover letter is concise—no more than three or four paragraphs—and informative. You want to quickly show the hiring manager how your experience makes you a good candidate for the job. Start with a paragraph stating why you are writing, what job you are seeking, and where you heard about it. In the next paragraph or two, move on to discuss your skills and experience and how they relate directly to the job requirements. Close with a short paragraph that thanks the reader and says what you plan to do to follow up on your application, such as "I hope to hear from you soon."

Should you discuss salary in a cover letter? No. For most health care jobs, the salary range or hourly rate is narrow and there is not a lot of room to negotiate. Whatever range is given in the job description is pretty much what the job will pay. Before you apply, research the job to be sure the salary is within your range. If no salary is given, do a little research to find the approximate rate for your skills and experience level at other nearby employers.

Health Care Job Interviews

When you reach the point of an interview, congratulate yourself—you have already made it past a lot of hurdles and are now at the point where the employer is giving serious consideration to hiring you. Being well prepared is the best way to be sure of making a good impression at this crucial step. Review again why your skills and interests relate well to the job.

A health care job interview is a two-way process—the questions go both ways. The goal is decide if the job is a good match for you both. You want to convince the employer that you are the best person for the job and that you will fit in well with the rest of the staff. You want the employer to convince you of the same thing. The interview will often start with open-ended questions such as "Tell me about yourself" or "Why are you interested in our organization?" Even though the questions are open-ended, try to focus your answers and keep them short. You might reply to "Tell me about yourself" by saying "I am an experienced cardiac technician. I have an AA degree and have special expertise in thallium stress tests. I am looking for a job that will let me use my skills in a more fast-paced environment." To answer, "Why are you interested in our organization?", it helps to have done your research first. Respond by mentioning the

Professional
Ethics

Patient Privacy

Patient privacy is a very serious matter. It is strictly regulated by HIPAA and the rules apply to everyone with access to patient records, even receptionists and the billing department. Violating the rules is grounds for being fired. The temptation to take an unauthorized peek at a patient record—and to reveal that information to the press—can be strong, especially when a celebrity is involved. Resist the temptation! Violating privacy rules is grounds for immediate firing. That is what happened to fifteen California hospital workers in 2009 when they took unauthorized looks at the medical records for the famous octuplet mother.

organization's special mission, how it is a leader in your area, how that gives you an opportunity to develop your skills, and so on.

If you are just starting your health care career, by definition you do not have much job experience. Do not apologize for this. Instead, emphasize your training, your willingness to work hard and gradually take on responsibility, and your desire to learn. Talk about how the job relates to an area that interests you—working with patients with movement disorders, for instance. If you do have relevant experience from other jobs, be sure to mention it. For example, if you worked in a day care center and are now looking for your first LPN job, you can say that you have a lot of experience with small children and in communicating clearly with parents. That gives you an edge for a job in the pediatrics department.

Interviewers for health care jobs love to ask you behavioral questions to learn how you respond to specific situations. A typical question might be, "Tell me about how you handled a situation with an angry member of a patient's family." Another typical question might be, "What's the most challenging patient experience you have ever had?" There are not any set answers to these questions—the interviewer just wants to get an idea of what you did and thought in a key situation. Describe the situation briefly, and emphasize specifically how you found a positive resolution. And if you did not, be honest and say what you learned from the experience and how you did better the next time.

You get to ask questions at an interview, too. Before the interview, work out a short list of the questions that are most important to you (but do not ask about salary and benefits). Typical questions you might want to ask include:

➡ What are the main tasks of this job?

➡ Who will I report to?

➡ How is performance evaluated and how often?

➡ How does this job fit into the bigger organizational structure?

➡ What are the training opportunities?

➡ What could I expect to be doing six months after starting this job?

If you are not happy with some of the answers, it could be this is not the right job for you. No matter how you feel, keep the interview positive and upbeat. Ask what the next step will be and thank the interviewer for his or her time.

Let us assume you make a good impression at the first interview. You might get an offer on the spot, though it is more likely you will get a phone call within a week or two. For many professional-level positions in health care, though, the process takes longer. The next step is often a selection interview, where you are asked to come back to meet with the hiring supervisor—usually someone a step above whoever you interviewed with the first time. The hiring supervisor is looking for reasons to keep you in the running for the job. Help him or her along by being enthusiastic about the position and knowledgeable about the institution. Emphasize again your education, training, and experience, and try to come across as confident and assured. If all goes well, this will be your last interview and a job offer will soon follow.

As you move up in your career to more senior jobs, the interviewing process gets even more complicated. If you are interviewing for a position as a nurse manager, for example, you might be asked to do a series interview, where you meet several different staff members (your future colleagues) individually one after the other. Treat each interview as if it were your first—you still need to make a good impression, ask intelligent questions, and show how your skills are a good fit for the job.

A variation on the series interview is the panel interview, where you meet with several staff members at once. A panel interview can be very stressful, because you are outnumbered and the questions come quickly. Try to stay calm and focused. Make eye contact and give your answers to the whole panel, not just the person asking the question. Take advantage of the situation to see how the staff members behave individually and how they work together—this can give you valuable clues about how it might be to work with them yourself.

After each interview, make notes to yourself about the people you met and what they told you about the job. Evaluate yourself on how well you answered the questions. If you feel you did not do well, ask yourself how you could do better. Make a list of the questions you did not get to ask—if you get a call back, you will know what questions you still want answered. Most importantly, ask yourself if you want to get a job offer from this employer. Do not waste time by following up on jobs that do not interest you or where it is clear you are not the right person. Do, however, always write thank-you notes to everyone you meet.

Is This Employer Right for You?

As a health care worker, you want to do what is right for your patients and also advance in your career. Those two things will happen best if your potential employer puts a premium on quality, safety, collaboration, continuity of care, and accountability. As a practical matter, there are some questions you should ask to be sure the employer is right for you:

➡ What is the ratio of nurses (or whatever your area is) to patients?

➡ What support staff are available to assist?

➡ How are staff members held accountable for high-quality care?

➡ What are the opportunities for professional growth?

➡ Does my department collaborate with other departments to provide patient care and work on improvements to care quality?

➡ How long has the average professional in my department been with you?

Positive answers to questions like these tell you the employer is serious about providing quality health care—and that the institution is likely to be a good place to work.

Returning to the Health Care Workforce

Every year many individuals leave the health care workforce to do something else, such as raise their families, work in another area, or even retire. If they are out of the workforce long enough, they may have let their license or certification lapse. Health care moves fast. If you are out of the field for too long, your skills and knowledge might be too far behind the times to make you employable.

What if you still want to go back your former career in health care? It might be easier than you think, even if your license has not been renewed and you have been out of the field for several years or even longer. Today the demand for health care providers, especially registered nurses, is so large that many community colleges, nursing schools, and even large medical centers offer refresher courses designed to brush up your rusty skills and bring you up to speed on new medical developments. Many state licensing agencies are making special efforts to help nurses and LPNs restore lapsed licenses. Do not give up on returning to health care until you have explored this option.

Chapter 5

Talk Like a Pro

The language of health care is complex—it is why medical dictionaries are thousands of pages long. You will learn the specialized vocabulary you need for your particular health care skill in the classroom and in your clinical training. This chapter helps you sort out the many professional associations, certification abbreviations, and general medical terminology that will help you understand the bigger picture of day-to-day work in a hospital, nursing home, doctors' office, or other health care setting.

AACN American Academy of Nurse Practitioners.

AA degree Associate's degree.

AANA American Association of Nurse Anesthetists.

AART American Registry of Radiologic Technologists.

ABHES Accrediting Bureau of Health Education Schools.

abstract Short summary of a medical or technical article, giving the main points and the conclusion.

academic medical center Medical complex combining patient care with medical education and consisting of a medical school, university hospital, affiliated teaching hospitals, clinics, libraries, and other facilities.

accreditation A decision by an authorized credentialing body that an institution, program, or individual meets the high professional standards set by the body.

Accreditation Review Committee on Education in Surgical Technology (ARC-ST)   Accrediting agency for surgical technologists.

Accrediting Bureau of Health Education Schools (ABHES)   Accrediting agency for schools of allied health, including vocational schools and technical institutes.

ACLS   Advanced Cardiovascular Life Support certification from the American Heart Association. Because this program teaches CPR, it is a requirement for many health care jobs.

activities of daily living (ADL)   The normal activities of a healthy individual, such as eating, getting dressed, bathing, and so on.

acupuncture   The practice of inserting very fine needles through the skin at specific points for the purpose of treating disease or relieving pain; originally a Chinese practice now widely used in alternative medicine.

acute   An illness that has a sudden onset, sharp rise, and short duration, such as a kidney stone or appendicitis; characterized by sharpness or severity, as in acute pain.

acute care   Short-term medical care for serious acute disease, such as a kidney stone, or serious trauma

ADA   American Dietetic Association; American Dental Association.

ADA   Americans with Disabilities Act.

ADE   Adverse drug event.

ADL   Activities of daily living.

ADR   Adverse drug reaction.

advanced life support (ALS)   Emergency treatment to open airways, maintain blood pressure, respiration, and pulse, and other measures administered by a paramedic.

advanced practice nurse (APN)   A registered nurse who has taken additional training beyond nursing school and has a master's degree in nursing. APNs include nurse practitioners, clinical nurse specialists, and certified registered nurse anesthetists.

adverse drug event (ADE)   A bad reaction by a patient to a drug, often a prescribed medication.

adverse drug reaction (ADR)   A bad reaction by a patient to a drug, often a prescribed medication.

adverse health care event   Anything that goes wrong in the treatment of a patient, including an adverse drug reaction, medical error, or patient-caused problem such as failure to take prescribed medication or follow medical advice.

Everyone

Knows

Calling a Code

Emergency codes are used in a hospital to alert the staff to emergency situations, such a patient in cardiac arrest or a problem such as a fire or bomb threat, without panicking patients and visitors. Depending on the code, staff members know exactly what they are expected to do. Codes are usually described by color, though some other codes are also used. Codes vary somewhat from hospital to hospital, so the list below may not always apply in all situations. Calling a code means to announce the code; the patient who needs the emergency help is said to be coding. As a health care worker, you need to be aware of the codes used in your hospital and what you are supposed to do when one is called.

Code Amber Infant or child abduction

Code Blue Patient in need of immediate resuscitation, usually due to cardiac arrest. Also more generally used to mean any adult medical emergency. Because code blue is so widely known to the public, many hospitals now substitute a private code.

Code Pink Medical emergency involving a pregnant woman or newborn.

Code Red Fire.

Code Silver Violent situation, often involving a combative person or a weapon.

Code Trauma Alerts trauma team that a patient is arriving shortly.

Code White Medical emergency involving a child.

AHDI Association for Healthcare Documentation Integrity, an organization for health information technology workers.

allied health careers All the many different health care jobs, such as nurse, occupational therapist, medical transcriptionist, or radiological technologist that support the work of doctors and dentists.

allopathic Standard medical practice, using all treatments that have been shown to help treat disease.

alternative medicine   Healing or treatment systems, such
as homeopathy, naturopathy, or faith healing, that are not
standard medical practice and are not traditionally taught in
medical schools.

ALS   Advanced life support.

ambulatory care   Health care provided to patients who are well
enough to arrive at the treatment center on their own.

ambulatory surgery center   Specialized medical center
providing nonemergency surgery to patients who are well
enough to arrive on their own and who will not need
hospitalization following the surgery.

American Academy of Nurse Practitioners   Professional and
certifying association for nurse practitioners.

American Academy of Nurse Practitioners Certifying Board
National certifying agency for nurse practitioners.

American Dental Association (ADA)   National professional
and certifying association for dentists and dental hygienists.

American Dietetic Association (ADA)   National professional
and certifying association for dietitians, dietetic technicians
registered, and nutritionists.

American Medical Technologists (AMT)   Certifying agency
for medical assistants.

American Physical Therapy Association (APTA)   National
professional and certifying association for physical therapists.

**American Registry of Diagnostic Medical Sonographers
(ARDMS)**   Credentialing agency for cardiovascular technology,
including vascular technology and diagnostic cardiac sonography.

American Registry of Radiologic Technologists (AART)
National credentialing agency for radiologic technologists.

American Speech-Language-Hearing Association (ASHA)
National professional and certifying association for speech-
language pathologists and audiologists.

Americans with Disabilities Act (ADA)   Federal law
mandating equal opportunity for persons with disabilities,
including access to medical services.

AMT   American Medical Technologists, professional organization
for medical assistants.

APN   Advanced practice nurse.

APTA   American Physical Therapy Association.

ARC-ST   Accreditation Review Committee on Education in
Surgical Technology.

ARDMS American Registry of Diagnostic Medical Sonographers.

ASHA American Speech-Language-Hearing Association, professional organization for speech-language pathologists and audiologists.

Association for Healthcare Documentation Integrity (AHDI) The national certifying agency for medical transcriptionists.

Association of Surgical Technologists (AST) National professional and credentialing agency for surgical technologists.

assisted living A residential facility that combines housing, support services, personal assistance, and health care for people who need help with the activities of daily living.

associate's degree (AA) Degree awarded after two years of fulltime academic study beyond high school

AST Association of Surgical Technologists.

attending physician Doctor in charge of a hospitalized patient's care.

AuD Doctor of Audiology.

audiologist Licensed health care professional who treats people with hearing problems and hearing loss.

audiology The area of health care dealing with hearing and treating people with impaired hearing.

BA degree Bachelor of arts degree.

bachelor's degree (BA or BS) Degree awarded after four or sometimes five years of fulltime academic study at a college or university.

biohazard A danger or potential danger caused by a biological agent, such as an infectious organism. Biohazard materials, such as used needles, discarded blood samples, and bandages, must be disposed of in a secure biohazard container.

board certified A nurse or PA who has passed examinations in a specialty area sponsored by a national governing association such as the Pediatric Nursing Certification Board

board of nursing (BON) In most states, the agency that licenses registered nurses, LPNs, LVNs, and some other health care professionals.

BS degree Bachelor of science degree.

BSN degree Bachelor of science nursing degree.

CAA Council on Academic Accreditation in Audiology and Speech-Language Pathology.

CAAHEP Committee on Accreditation for Allied Health Education Programs.

CADE   Commission on Accreditation for Dietetics Education.

CAM   Complementary and alternative medicine.

Cardiovascular Credentialing International (CCI)   Credentialing agency for cardiovascular technology, including vascular technology and diagnostic cardiac sonography.

case manager   Registered nurse assigned to coordinate and manage a patient's care throughout hospitalization and also to plan for the patient's discharge.

CCC-A   Certificate of clinical competence in audiology.

CCI   Cardiovascular Credentialing International.

CCRN   Critical care registered nurse.

CCU   Coronary care unit.

CDA   Certified dental assistant.

CDR   Commission on Dietetic Registration.

CE   Continuing education.

CEN   Certified emergency nurse.

Center for Medicaid and Medicare Services (CMS)   Agency that administers Medicaid and Medicare and is responsible for setting standards for any organization that receives reimbursement for services under these programs.

center of excellence   A health facility, department, or clinical service area that has a reputation for outstanding quality of care.

certification   Evaluation and recognition of an institution, program, or individual meeting high standards or requirements as set by a national or state certifying body.

certified dental assistant (CDA)   Dental assistant who has passed the certification requirements of the Dental Assisting National Board (DANB).

certified home health agency (CHHA)   Agency approved by the Center for Medicaid and Medicare Services to provide home health aides to clients.

certified medical transcriptionist (CMT)   Medical transcriptionist who has passed the advanced certifying exam of the Association for Healthcare Documentation Integrity (AHDI).

certified nurse midwife (CNM)   A registered nurse who has received advanced training in caring for women during pregnancy and childbirth and is certified by the American College of Nurse Midwives.

certified nursing assistant (CNA)   Individual trained to assist residents of nursing homes and residential care facilities with activities of daily living such as eating, grooming, and dressing. CNAs work under the supervision of a registered nurse.

certified occupational therapist assistant (COTA) Occupational therapist assistant certified by the National Board for Certification in Occupational Therapy.

certified registered nurse anesthetist (CRNA) An advanced practice nurse trained to prepare patients for procedures, administer anesthesia, and oversee recovery from anesthesia.

certified respiratory therapist (CRT) Respiratory therapist who has passed the certification exam of the National Board for Respiratory Care.

CGFNS Commission on Graduates of Foreign Nursing Schools.

CGFNS exam Test of nursing and English language skills for foreign-trained nurses; administered by Commission on Graduates of Foreign Nursing Schools. This exam is not a licensing or certification test, but it is good practice for the NCLEX test.

charge nurse Registered nurse responsible for overseeing nursing care on a unit during a particular shift.

chart The permanent medical record of a patient; to chart is to maintain and update the chart.

CHHA Certified home health agency.

clerkship Training position in hospital procedures for second- and third-year medical students.

clinic An outpatient medical center for diagnosis and treatment; usually connected to a hospital or medical school.

clinical Involving the direct observation and treatment of patients; related to or characterized by observable symptoms of disease.

clinical experience Practical training working directly with patients in a hospital or other health care setting.

clinical fellow Post-resident doctor receiving advanced training in a specialty at a hospital.

clinical laboratory technician (CLT) Laboratory professional who has a two-year degree from an accredited program and has passed a certification exam.

clinical nurse specialist (CNS) Registered nurse who has a master's degree and additional training and skills in physical diagnosis, patient assessment, and management of patient needs in primary care.

clinical operation manager *see* nurse manager.

Problem

Solving

Overcoming Language Barriers

When you and your patient do not have a language in common, you will need to find a way to communicate. If no trained interpreter or bilingual health care worker is available, you will have to turn to informal interpreters. In a large medical center there is often a language bank—a list of employees who speak a foreign language or who know American Sign Language (ASL). Some of them will not be health care workers, however, and they may not have the vocabulary to translate medical terms. Family members or friends can often serve as informal interpreters, but they too may not understand medical terms. When children are the interpreters, it is very difficult for them to understand and translate questions about adult issues such as rape or sexually transmitted disease. To help with language barriers, many health care centers now have written materials that put English questions and statements next to equivalents in the foreign language. Providers and patients can then communicating by pointing to the relevant words. It is not ideal, but particularly in an emergency, this is an effective technique.

CLT   Clinical laboratory technician.

CMT   Certified medical transcriptionist.

CNA   Certified nursing assistant.

CNM   Certified nurse-midwife.

CNS   Clinical nurse specialist.

Commission on Accreditation for Dietetics Education (CADE)   The accrediting agency of the American Dietetics Association for educational programs.

Commission on Accreditation of Allied Health Education Programs (CAAHEP)   National accrediting agency for most allied health education programs. Training programs that are not accredited by CAAHEP may not be acceptable to state licensing agencies or to employers.

Commission on Accreditation of Education Programs for the EMS Professions   Accrediting agency for EMS training programs.

Commission on Dietetic Registration (CDR)   Credentialing agency of the American Dietetic Association.

Commission on Graduates of Foreign Nursing Schools (CGFNS)   Agency that reviews the education of graduates of foreign nursing schools to be sure applicants meet an educational standard equivalent to an American-trained nurse.

communication disorder   A problem with speech, hearing, or language, such as stuttering, delays in speech and language, or autism.

community hospital   Any nonfederal hospital whose facilities and services are available to the public.

complementary medicine   Alternative medicine practices, such as acupuncture, that are sometimes used in standard medical treatment.

continuing competency   Learning activities such as those undertaken for the purpose of increasing and maintaining professional skills.

continuing education   Formal classes, workshops, or self-study activities that carry continuing education units or hours and are offered by approved sponsors.

continuing professional development   Learning activities such as those undertaken for the purpose of increasing and maintaining professional skills.

co-pay   Portion of the payment for an office visit or medical service paid by the patient; the remainder is paid by the insurance company, Medicaid, or Medicare; usually in the range of $5 to $40.

coronary care unit (CCU)   Specialized area of a hospital for treating patients with heart disease.

COTA   Certified occupational therapist assistant.

Council on Academic Accreditation in Audiology and Speech-Language Pathology (CAA)   Accrediting agency for academic programs in audiology and speech-language pathology.

CPD   Continuing professional development.

CPM   Certified professional midwife.

CPR   Cardiopulmonary resuscitation, a procedure used after cardiac arrest that includes mouth-to-mouth artificial respiration and heart massage by exerting pressure on the chest. Certification in CPR is usually a requirement for most health care workers.

CRNA Certified registered nurse anesthetist.

CRT Certified respiratory therapist.

critical Relating to an illness or condition involving the danger of death.

critical care Specialized hospital unit for the care of critically ill patients.

critical care registered nurse (CCRN) Registered nurse with advanced training in treating critically ill patients.

CST Certified surgical technologist.

CT Computed tomography, an imaging method using X-rays.

CT scan A three-dimensional image of the body created by computed tomography, a technique that uses a series of X-rays made along an axis and constructed by computer. Also called a CAT scan.

DANB Dental Assisting National Board.

DDS Doctor of dental surgery; a dentist.

deductible The portion of medical costs paid by the patient before insurance benefits begin.

Dental Assisting National Board (DANB) Certifying agency for dental assistants.

diagnosis Identifying a disease by its signs and symptoms; the conclusion reached by observing the patient, as in a diagnosis of bronchitis.

diagnostic imaging center Medical center specializing in providing images of the body, such as X-rays, MRIs, and CT scans.

diagnostic test A procedure, such as a blood test, used to determine the presence and extent of a disease and to identify it.

dietetic technician registered (DTR) Technician who has completed a two-year training program and an internship in nutrition and has passed the national registration exam given by the American Dietetic Association.

dietitian Registered dietitian.

director of nursing (DON) Registered nurse in charge of all nurses in a hospital or other facility. Replaces the old-fashioned term head nurse.

DNP Doctorate nurse practitioner.

DO Doctor of osteopathy.

doctoral degree Advanced degree, usually the PhD, awarded after at least three years of fulltime academic work beyond the bachelor's degree. Recipients of doctoral degrees are often addressed as Doctor, but they are not usually medical doctors.

doctor of naturopathy (ND)   A practitioner of naturopathy who has graduated from a training program at a naturopathic medical college.

doctor of osteopathy (DO)   A physician following a system of medicine that believes diseases are caused by a loss of structural integrity and can be treated by manipulation of the body in addition to therapeutic measures such as drugs or surgery. In modern medicine, DOs are basically indistinguishable from MDs.

DON   Director of nursing.

DTR   Dietetic technician, registered.

Dx   Medical shorthand for diagnosis.

echocardiography   The use of ultrasound to examine the heart and to diagnose abnormalities and disease.

ED   Emergency department.

EHR   Electronic health record.

emergency department (ED)   Emergency room.

emergency medical services (EMS)   Out-of-hospital acute medical care for patients with illnesses or injuries that are a medical emergency, and/or ambulance or other transport to a hospital for further treatment.

emergency room (ER)   Specialized section of a hospital devoted to rapid treatment of patients with urgent illnesses or injuries.

EMS   Emergency medical services, including ambulance service and other first responders such as rescue squads.

EMT   Emergency medical technician.

EMT-B   EMT basic.

EMT-Basic   Second skill level for emergency medical workers, above the EMT level ; the national licensing exam taken by all EMTs who have completed EMT basic training. Administered by Commission on Accreditation of Education Programs for the EMS Professions.

EMT-I   EMT intermediate.

EMT-Intermediate   Third skill level for emergency medical workers; the national licensing exam taken by all EMTs who have completed EMT basic training. Administered by Commission on Accreditation of Education Programs for the EMS Professions.

EMT-P   Paramedic.

encounter   Any meeting with a patient in an outpatient therapeutic setting, such as at the doctor's office or in the emergency room.

ER   Emergency room, also sometimes called emergency department.

FDA   Food and Drug Administration, the federal agency that approves and regulates the use of drugs.

fellow   Doctor who has complete medical school and residency training and is getting additional training in particular specialty such as heart surgery.

first responder   First skill level for emergency medical workers.

floater   A health care worker who is assigned as needed to different units of a hospital or clinic, rather than having a single permanent assignment.

floating   The practice of temporarily reassigning a health care worker to a different unit in hospital or clinic.

formulary   A list of drugs approved for use in a hospital, clinic, or other medical practice; the list of drugs approved for reimbursement by a health insurance company.

geriatric   Relating to the health problems and diseases of aging and old age.

geriatrics   The branch of medicine dealing with the health problems and diseases of aging and old age.

graduate nursing education   Nurse education programs leading to a master's or doctorate degree.

grand rounds   Rounds by an expert doctor on a clinical issue, accompanied by hospital medical staff.

health educator   Certified health care worker who teaches patients about a particular health condition, such as diabetes or asthma, and how to manage it.

health management organization (HMO)   A managed care organization that is both insurer and provider of health care services in exchange for prepaid payments.

Health on the Net Foundation (HON)   International organization that sets standards for accuracy and ethics for health-related Web sites. Sites that meet the standard are allowed to place the HONcode logo on their pages.

HIPAA   Health Insurance Portability and Accountability Act, the federal legislation that mandates the privacy of patient health records. Pronounced hippa.

history   An overall account of a patient's family and personal health background and his or her past and current health; the past and present of a patient's particular health problem.

HMO   Health management organization.

home health services   Nursing, therapy, and health-related homemaker and social services provided in the patient's home.

homeopath   A practitioner of homeopathy.

homeopathy   A medical belief system that treats disease by administering very tiny doses of a substance that would, in a healthy person, produce symptoms similar to the disease.

HON   Health on the Net Foundation.

HON code   Certification that a Web site follows the ethical code of the Health on the Net Foundation.

hospice   Inpatient or home program providing palliative care and support services for terminally ill patients and their families.

hospital   A organization or corporate entity licensed by a state to provide diagnostic and therapeutic patient services for a variety of medical conditions.

hospitalist   Attending physician who cares only for patients in the hospital.

ICD-9   International Classification of Diseases, ninth edition. Official codes for diagnoses; the standard reference work for medical coding and billing.

ICU   Intensive care unit.

IDEA   Individuals with Disabilities Education Act.

Individuals with Disabilities Education Act (IDEA)   The federal law that mandates a free and appropriate education for children and young adults with disabilities.

infection control   Procedures, such as frequent hand washing or wearing gloves and sterile gowns, to limit the spread of infection from one person to another.

inpatient   A patient who has been admitted to a hospital for treatment; referring to services and treatment provided to hospitalized patients.

in-service education   Classes, seminars, and training programs provided to hospital, clinic, and other staff members during working hours as part of the job.

intensive care unit (ICU)   A specialized area of a hospital for treating patients who are gravely ill.

intensivist   An attending physician who only treats patients in the intensive care unit (ICU).

intern   Physician who has just graduated from medical school and is being trained at the hospital; interns work with attending physicians to provide patient care.

internist   Physician specializing in internal medicine, the branch of medicine that deals with the diagnosis and nonsurgical treatment of diseases affecting adults.

internship   Supervised clinical work with patients in a hospital or other setting as part of a student's training; often a required part of training for dietitians, physical therapists, and others who provide direct patient care.

invasive   A medical procedure, such as surgery or an imaging technique that requires the injection of a dye, that involves entering the body.

IV   Intravenous, or administered through a vein; usually refers to an intravenous infusion of fluids or drugs.

JCAHO   Joint Commission on the Accreditation of Healthcare Organizations.

Joint Commission on the Accreditation of Healthcare Organizations (JCAHO)   The major national agency for accrediting hospitals and other healthcare organizations; JCAHO accreditation is necessary to be allowed to treat patients and receive Medicare, Medicaid, and health insurance reimbursement.

Joint Review Committee on Educational Programs in Nuclear Medicine Technology (JRCNMT)   Accrediting agency for approved nuclear technologist training programs.

Joint Review Committee on Education in Diagnostic Medical Sonography (JRC-DMS)   Accrediting agency for approved diagnostic medical sonography training programs.

Joint Review Committee on Education in Radiologic Technology (JRCERT)   Accrediting agency for approved radiologic technology training programs.

JRC-DMS   Joint Review Committee on Education in Diagnostic Medical Sonography.

JRCERT   Joint Review Committee on Education in Radiologic Technology.

JRCNMT   Joint Review Committee on Educational Programs in Nuclear Medicine Technology.

level-one trauma center   A well-equipped hospital with specially trained staff, designated as a regional center for receiving and treating severely injured or ill patients.

Everyone
Knows

Medical Slang

There are a *lot* of slang expressions in health care. Many of them are jokingly insulting, either to patients or fellow health care workers, some are sexist, and a lot of them cannot be included in a book that children might see. You will just have to learn them on the job. The list below includes some of the more acceptable medical slang terms.

adminisphere   Where the hospital management works.

AOB   Alcohol on board, said of an intoxicated patient

appy   A patient with appendicitis.

baby catcher   Obstetrician or midwife.

banana bag   An IV bag containing fluids, electrolytes, vitamins, and minerals, named for the yellow color of the contents.

cabbage   Heart bypass operation, from CABG meaning coronary artery bypass graft.

circling the drain   Nearing death.

doughnut   CT scanner.

Foley   A catheter used to drain urine from the bladder.

gas passer   An anesthetist.

house red   Blood.

M & Ms   Mortality and morbidity conferences, where doctors discuss difficult cases, medical mistakes, and patient deaths. Also called death and doughnuts, because doughnuts and coffee are traditionally served.

shotgunning   Ordering a wide variety of medical tests because the doctor is not sure what's wrong with the patient.

stat   Immediately, at once, as soon as possible.

tox screen   Blood tests to find the type and level of drugs in a patient's system.

UBI   Unexplained beer injury, said when an intoxicated patient cannot explain how he or she got hurt.

level-two trauma center   A regional trauma center providing higher levels of specialized care, such as a burn center or neonatal intensive care unit.

licensed practical nurse   Licensed health care worker who assists patients with tasks such as bathing, changing wound dressings, and taking vital signs. LPNs have at least one year of training and must be licensed by their state to practice.lLicensed vocational nurse. The title used in the states of Texas and California for licensed practical nurse.

licensure   The legal right, usually conferred by a state or accrediting body, to engage in certain professions (licensed practical nurse, for example) or to operate certain types of health-care facilities (nursing home, for example).

limited English proficient (LEP)   An individual who does not speak or understand English well.

limited service provider   Hospital or ambulatory care facility focusing on a specific service or group of services, such as open heart surgery.

long-term care facility   A residential facility, such as a nursing home or rehabilitation center, caring for patients who need continuing care.

LPN   Licensed practical nurse.

LTC   Long-term care.

LVN   Licensed vocational nurse.

magnet hospital   Hospital recognized by the American Nurses Credentialing Center for providing sustained excellence in nursing care; a hospital that is very attractive to nurses as place to work.

magnetic resonance imaging (MRI)   A noninvasive diagnostic technique that produces computerized images of internal body tissues. It uses radio waves, not a radioactive material, to induce nuclear magnetic resonance of atoms.

managed care   A broad range of ways to provide health care delivery and financing, including health management organizations and preferred provider organizations.

master's degree   Advanced degree awarded after one to two years of fulltime academic study beyond a bachelor's degree.

MD   Medical doctor.

Medicaid   Medical aid for those unable to afford health insurance or medical care; funded jointly by the state and federal governments.

medical doctor (MD)   A highly skilled health care professional licensed to practice medicine.

medical laboratory technician (MLT)   Laboratory professional who has a two-year degree from an accredited program and has passed a certification exam.

medically underserved area (MUA)   An area, often rural or inner-city, where residents have a shortage of personal health services.

medical student   A student studying to become a doctor. Medical students spend the last two years of their training working in the hospital and seeing patients under the close supervision of residents and attending physicians.

medical transcriptionist   A person who converts dictated reports from doctors and others into written records.

Medicare   The federal government program that pays for medical care, especially for the elderly.

meds   Slang for medications.

mentor   An experienced individual who acts as an advisor, guide, or coach for someone who is new to an employer or profession.

MLT   Medical laboratory technician.

MRI   Magnetic resonance imaging.

MS   Master of science degree.

MUA   Medically underserved area.

NAEMT   National Association of Emergency Medical Technicians.

National Association of Emergency Medical Technicians (NAEMT)   National membership and credentialing association for EMTs and paramedics.

National Board for Certification in Occupational Therapy   Accrediting agency for occupational therapists and occupational therapy assistants.

National Board for Respiratory Care (NBRC)   Certifying agency for respiratory therapists.

National Board of Surgical Technology and Surgical Assisting (NBSTSA)   Certifying agency for surgical technologists.

National Commission for Certifying Agencies (NCCA)   Accrediting agency for some health care professions, particularly in nursing.

National Commission on Certification of Physician Assistants (NCCPA)   Certifying agency for physician assistants.

National Credentialing Agency for Laboratory Personnel (NCA) National agency for certification of medical lab workers.

National Registry of Emergency Medical Technicians National certifying and registry agency for emergency medical technicians and paramedics.

naturopath A practitioner of naturopathy.

naturopathy A system that focuses on natural agents, such as herbal remedies, and physical methods, such as acupuncture and massage, to treat disease.

NBRC National Board for Respiratory Care.

NBSTSA National Board of Surgical Technology and Surgical Assisting.

NCA National Credentialing Agency for Laboratory Personnel.

NCCA National Commission for Certifying Agencies (NCCA).

NCCPA National Commission on Certification of Physician Assistants.

NCLEX-PN National Council Licensure Examination for Practical Nurses; the national written exam all LPNs must pass to be licensed.

NCLEX-RN National Council Licensure Examination for Registered Nurses; the national written exam all RNs must pass to be licensed.

ND Doctor of naturopathy.

network A group of hospitals, doctors, other health providers, and sometimes community agencies working together to coordinate and deliver health care services to the community.

never event A medical error so serious it should never occur; an example would be giving a drug intravenously when it should be given by mouth.

NLC Nurse licensure compact, an agreement among a number of states to honor nursing licenses across state lines.

NMTCB Nuclear Medicine Technology Certification Board.

noninvasive A medical procedure, such as taking an X-ray, that does not involve entering the body.

NP Nurse practitioner.

NP-C Certified nurse practitioner.

NREMT National Registry of Emergency Medical Technicians.

Nuclear Medicine Technology Certification Board (NMTCB) Credentialing agency for nuclear medicine technologists.

NUM Nurse unit manager.

nurse unit manager (NUM) The registered nurse in charge of a hospital unit during his or her shift.

nurse midwife Registered nurse with advanced training in caring for women during pregnancy and childbirth.

nurse practitioner Registered nurse with additional training and skills in physical diagnosis, patient assessment, and management of patient needs in primary care. NPs hold master's degrees, are board-certified in their specialty, and are licensed by the state where they work.

nursing home Long-term residential facility for individuals, usually elderly, who need continuous skilled nursing care.

nutritionist Someone who provides nutritional advice. In some states nutritionists are certified or licensed; in others, there are few requirements. See Registered dietitian.

occupational therapist (OT) Licensed health care worker who helps patients improve coordination and motor skills important for activities of daily living.

occupational therapist assistant (OTA) Health care worker who assists an occupational therapist.

occupational therapist registered (OTR) Occupational therapist certified by the National Board for Certification in Occupational Therapy.

on call Being available to come in to work on short notice if necessary.

OSHA Occupational Safety and Health Administration, the main federal agency in charge of setting and enforcing safety regulations in the workplace.

osteopathy A system of medicine based on the theory that diseases are caused by a loss of structural integrity and can be treated by manipulation of the body in addition to therapeutic measures such as drugs or surgery.

OT Occupational therapist.

OTA Occupational therapist assistant.

OTR Occupational therapist registered.

outpatient A patient who is treated at a hospital, clinic, or other health care center and does not need to be admitted to the hospital.

outpatient care center A health care center providing specialized treatment on an outpatient or day basis, such as a dialysis center or substance abuse treatment center.

Everyone
Knows

Prescription Abbreviations

Doctors, nurse practitioners, and physician assistants often use abbreviations, usually based on Latin terms, when they write a prescription, called a script, for short. (The symbol Rx for a prescription comes from the Latin word *recipe*, meaning "take.") As a health care worker, it is your job to understand these abbreviations and explain them to patients. The list below gives some of the most common abbreviations, their Latin origins where relevant, and what they mean.

a.c. *Ante cibum*; before meals.

a.d. *Auris dextra*; right ear.

amp Ampule, a small container holding a liquid or powder that is added to water to make the drug dose.

amt Amount.

a.l. *Auris laeva*; left ear.

a.s. *Auris sinistra*; left ear.

bis *Bis*; twice.

b.d. or b.i.d. *Bis in die*; twice daily.

cap. Capsule.

cc *Cum cibo*; with food.

D.A.W. Dispense as written, instead of using a generic drug.

g Gram.

h.s. *Hora somni*; at bedtime.

IM Intramuscular injection.

inj. Injection.

IV Intravenous.

mg Milligram.

nebul *Nebula*; a spray.

o_2 Both eyes.

o.d. *Oculus dexter*; right eye.

o.s. *Oculus sinister; left eye.*

p.c. *Post cibum*; after meals.

prn *Pro re nata*; as needed.

p.o. *Per os*; by mouth or orally.

q.d. *Quaque die*; every day.

q.i.d. *Quater quaque hora*; every four hours.

tab Tablet.

t.i.d. *Ter in die*; three times a day.

U.S.P. United States Pharmacopoeia, standard reference book for drug names

PA   Physician assistant.

PA-C   Physician assistant certified.

palliative care   Medical care focusing on pain control and comfort for terminal patients.

PANCE   Physician Assistant National Certifying Exam.

PANRE   Physician Assistant National Recertifying Exam.

paramedic   Emergency medical services worker qualified to administer drugs and perform some medical procedures.

paraprofessional   A trained health care provider who works alongside physicians and others to assist with treatment and perform basic procedures and tasks.

patient advocate   A hospital or nursing home staff member assigned to represent patients and ensure they are receiving quality care.

patient assistance programs   Pharmaceutical industry programs providing low-cost or free drugs to needy patients.

patient encounter   Any meeting with a patient outside of inpatient care.

PCP   Primary care physician.

pediatrics   The branch of medicine dealing with the health problems of children. Often shortened to "peds," pronounced peeds.

personal health record (PHR)   An individual's electronic health record, stored on a computer.

pharmacist   Licensed health care professional providing medications for patients. Hospital pharmacists work with the medical team to choose appropriate medications.

pharmacy technician   Healthcare worker assisting pharmacists.

Ph.D.   Doctoral degree.

phlebotomist   Health care worker trained in drawing blood from patients.

PHR   Personal health record, an electronic health record stored on a computer.

physical therapist (PT)   Licensed health care worker who works with patients to improve mobility, decrease pain, and reduce disability caused by illness or injury.

physical therapist assistant (PTA)   Healthcare worker who assists a physical therapist.

physician assistant (PA)   Healthcare professional licensed to practice medicine under physician supervision.

physician assistant certified (PA-C)   Physician assistant who
has passed the test administered by the National Commission on
Certification of Physician Assistants.

portability   Allowing state-licensed or state-certified health care
workers, such as registered nurse, to work in other states without
needing to obtain a license there. Regulations vary substantially
from state to state and portability often does not apply.

post baccalaureate   Academic study after receiving a bachelor's
degree, often in preparation for applying to a program offering
an advanced degree.

PPO   Preferred provider organization.

PubMed   Integrated online search and retrieval system for
biomedical literature. It provides free access to abstracts and
often also to full articles from thousands of medical journals.

practicum   A hands-on course designed to train health care
workers in the clinical application of material learned in the
classroom.

preceptor   An experienced health care worker assigned to mentor
a recent graduate during his or her first year on the job.

preferred provider organization (PPO)   A type of managed
care where a group of providers agree to offer health services
to participating patients covered by a particular insurance
company or employer.

primary care   Basic health services such as preventive care,
health screenings, check-ups, and the diagnosis and treatment
of common health problems. Usually provided in a doctor's
office or clinic by primary care physicians, nurse practitioners,
and physician assistants.

primary care hospital   Hospital that offers emergency care
and basic services but has limited facilities for intensive or
specialized care.

primary care physician (PCP)   A doctor providing primary
care services such as preventive care, health screenings, and
diagnosis and treatment of common health problems.

provider   Someone who delivers health-care services within the
scope of a professional license

PT   Physical therapist.

PTA   Physical therapy assistant.

radiology   The branch of medicine using nonradioactive energy,
such as X-rays and ultrasound, in the diagnosis and treatment of
disease.

RCS   Registered cardiac sonographer.

RD   Registered dietitian.

RDCS   Registered diagnostic cardiac sonographer.

RDH   Registered dental hygienist.

RDMS   Registered diagnostic medical sonographer.

registered cardiac sonographer (RCS)   Diagnostic medical sonographer specializing in imaging the heart and surrounding blood vessels.

registered dental hygienist (RDH)   Dental hygienist who has passed the national certification exam of the American Dental Association.

registered diagnostic cardiac sonographer (RDCS)   A cardiovascular technologist who performs cardiac sonography and is certified by the American Registry of Diagnostic Medical Sonographers (ARDMS).

registered diagnostic medical sonographer (RDMS)   Diagnostic medical sonographer who is certified by the American Registry of Diagnostic Medical Sonographers (ARDMS).

registered dietitian (RD)   Dietitian who has passed the certifying exam of the Commission on Dietetic Registration (CDR).

registered medical transcriptionist (RMT)   Medical transcriptionist who has passed the certifying exam of the Association for Healthcare Documentation Integrity (AHDI).

registered nurse   A nurse who has graduated from an approved training program, has received a state license, and is currently registered by the state where he or she works.

registered respiratory therapist (RRT)   Respiratory therapist who has passed the advanced certification exams of the National Board for Respiratory Care.

registration   Listing your name on a state registry of qualified professionals in your field.

registry   Database of present and past patients in a practice, clinic, hospital, nursing home, or other facility providing health care.

registry personnel   Temporary healthcare workers hired through an agency, not directly by the hospital or clinic.

rehabilitation   Therapy to help a sick or disabled person restore function and regain the ability to perform the activities of daily living.

rehabilitation center   Short-term residential facility where sick or disabled individuals receive therapy to restore function and help them regain the ability to perform the activities of daily living. Often shortened to rehab center.

resident   A doctor who has graduated from medical school and is now training in a specialty, such as cancer treatment. Residents are supervised by attending physicians, who must approve their decisions.

respiratory therapist (RT)   Licensed healthcare worker who evaluates, treats, and cares for people with breathing problems and other problems that affect the lungs.

RN   Registered nurse.

rotation   The practice of assigning health care personnel to different areas of the hospital on a regular basis.

rounds   A series of professional visits to patients in the hospital by a doctor or nurse.

RMT   Registered medical transcriptionist.

RRT   Registered respiratory therapist.

RT   Respiratory therapist.

Rx   Abbreviation for prescription.

SCHIP   State Children's Health Insurance Program, a federal program that provides fund to states for health insurance for children in families whose incomes are low but too high to qualify for Medicaid.

scope of practice   What treatments and other services a health care practitioner is allowed to perform based on the state's regulations and licensing provisions.

script   Medical slang for prescription.

scrubs   Simple, unadorned, collarless clothing worn as a uniform by health care workers.

shadowing   Following a staff member to learn more about how the job is done; used to help train new staff members and also to help people interested in health care learn more about a particular area.

sharps   Any object with a point or edge, such as a needle or scalpel, that must be disposed of in a special container to avoid contamination or injury.

skilled nursing facility (SNF)   An inpatient facility or unit, usually part of a hospital or nursing home, providing medical care, nursing, and other services under the supervision of a registered nurse.

SNF   Skilled nursing facility.

sonographer   Diagnostic medical sonographer.

sonography   Diagnostic or therapeutic use of ultrasound to image internal body structures and detect abnormalities.

special hospital   Hospital that provides services primarily in a specialized area such as obstetrics and gynecology or orthopedics.

speech-language pathologist   Licensed health care worker working with patients who have difficulty speaking or swallowing. Also called a speech-language therapist or just speech therapist. See also Audiologist.

staffing ratio   The number of registered nurses compared to the number of patients. The lower the ratio (in other words, if a nurse is assigned a small number of patients), the better the care. In intensive care units, the staffing ratio can be as low as 2:1, or one nurse for every two patients.

stat   Medical slang for immediately or right away. From the Latin statinum, meaning immediately.

teaching hospital   Hospital affiliated with a medical school or school of allied health offering training for medical students and residents, nursing students, or allied health students.

tertiary care hospital   Hospital providing specialty and subspecialty care not available in primary care hospitals.

Test of English as a Foreign Language (TOEFL)   Exam proving proficiency in written and spoken English; often required as a condition for licensing or certification for foreign-trained health care workers.

TOEFL   Test of English as a Foreign Language.

travel nurse   Registered nurse who works in temporary positions through an agency, not as an employee of the hospital or clinic.

trauma center   A hospital that provides emergency and specialized intensive care for critically ill and injured patients.

triage   Sorting patients according to the urgency of their need for care; used in emergency rooms and disaster scenes. Pronounced tree-AZH.

ultrasound   High-frequency sound vibrations used to image and examine internal body structures and detect abnormalities.

unit clerk   Hospital staff member providing clerical support to the nursing staff and direction to visitors. Also known at unit service assistant.

unit manager   Registered nurse in charge of a hospital floor or unit for the duration of a shift.

unit service assistant   Unit clerk.

urgent-care center A facility providing care for walk-in patients with illnesses or injuries that are not true medical emergencies.

vascular technologist Assists physician in the diagnosis and treatment of disorders affecting the blood vessels, usually using ultrasound instruments.

vocational certificate A certificate from a high school vocational program, a vocational school, or technical institute showing that the course of study has been completed.

X-ray Electromagnetic radiation with an extremely short wavelength that can penetrate solids and act on photographic films; the process of photographing with X-ray (to *x-ray*); the photograph produced by X-rays.

Chapter 6

Resources

Resources for getting started in health care and moving your career forward abound. Just about every aspect of health care has at least one professional society, credentialing body, accrediting agency, or some other organization dedicated to helping people enter the field, keep up with continuing education, and get the certifications that help you climb the career ladder.

Health care moves fast—and professionals need to keep up. Fortunately, there are also many, many resources that can help you stay on top of developments in your field through journals, Web sites, courses and seminars, online programs, and more.

To help you use this chapter, it starts with an overview of accrediting agencies and other associations and organizations dedicated to furthering health care as a career. The chapter moves on to some suggested reading for health care professionals and ends with a discussion of helpful Web sites.

To keep the list of accrediting agencies and professional groups to a manageable length, this section includes only national organizations. Many professions also have regional, state, and local organizations. Joining the professional organization for your specialty is important. The organization often have valuable information on its Web site, including job listings, notices of conferences and meetings, videos, and continuing education offerings. In addition, most professional organizations publish newsletters, magazines, and journals that help members keep up with new developments in the field. Being active in the local chapter of a national or state organization is also a great way to network with colleagues and take a leadership role.

The heading for books and periodicals lists classic and current titles that are worthwhile professional reading. However, there are so many professional journals within each health care profession that they cannot be listed here. A good starting point for finding journals, newsletters, and other periodicals that are relevant to you is the professional society for your area of health care.

In the Web sites section, we include a listing of reliable sources for health news and general health information. Patients often ask health care providers about things they learn in the media—it is important to keep up with health care news reports so you can give informed answers. Patients often also want to know more about their health problems. You may not have the time or expertise to give them detailed information. Instead, suggest a few reliable Web sites for learning more.

Associations and Organizations

These organizations and Web sites are an excellent starting point if you are considering a career in health care or want to move up in your current career. They are a valuable source of solid information about all the different career areas. Also check these sites for career advice, schools with accredited programs in health care, job listings, continuing medical education programs, virtual job fairs, and other information.

Broad-base Associations

This section lists the major overall credentialing agencies for health care education and training programs. Credentialing agencies for specific health care professions are listed under the relevant job title. Completing an accredited program is a requirement for state licensing and certification and for most forms of employment. Going on for additional certification from an accredited program is a big plus with employers. If a program is not accredited by one of these governing agencies or by a professional association, do not enroll in it. Your degree or certificate will probably not be acceptable to state licensing agencies or to employers.

Accrediting Bureau of Health Education Schools (ABHES) The ABHES assures the quality of the health care education programs it accredits through rigorous and systematic evaluation based on valid standards. 777 Leesburg Pike, Suite 314, North Falls Church, Virginia, 22043, (703) 917-9503 (http://www.abhes.org)

American Association of Colleges of Nursing (AACN) The national voice for baccalaureate and higher-degree nursing education programs, AACN's educational, research, governmental advocacy, data collection, publications, and other programs work to establish quality standards for bachelor's- and graduate-degree nursing education. Very informative Web site with a lot of information for those considering a career in nursing. One Dupont Circle NW, Suite 530, Washington, DC, 20036, (202) 463-6930 (http://www.aacn.nche.edu)

Commission on Accreditation of Allied Health Education Programs (CAAHEP) The largest programmatic accreditor in the health sciences field, CAAHEP reviews and accredits over two thousand educational programs in twenty health science

Problem
Solving

Evaluating Medical Web Sites

Medical information Web sites all too often contain information that is inaccurate, outdated, or misleading. You do not have time to waste chasing bad information; you may also have to cope with patients who have read bad information and are asking you about it. How can you determine if a medical Web site is trustworthy? Look for sites that have been approved by the Health on the Net (HON) Foundation. These sites carry the HONcode seal, indicating that they meet strict ethical standards such as clearly distinguishing advertising from editorial content, providing the professional qualifications of authors, and citing sources and dates of medical information. The vast majority of ethical, honest health Web sites participate in the HONcode program; be very cautious about relying on information from sites that do not carry the seal. For more information: http://www.hon.ch.

occupations. Look for CAAHEP accreditation as a minimum requirement for any worhtwhile health care education program. 1361 Park Street, Clearwater, Florida, 33756, (727) 210-2350 (http://www.caahep.org)

Commission on Graduates of Foreign Nursing Schools (CGFNS) CGFNS International is an internationally recognized authority on credentials evaluation and verification pertaining to the education, registration, and licensure of nurses and health care professionals worldwide. Foreign-trained nurses and health care workers will almost certainly need to work through CGFNs to have their credentials verified for admission offices and employers. Box 8628, Philadelphia, Pennsylvania, 19104, (215) 349-8767 (http://www.cgfns.org)

Specialty Associations

This section lists national professional associations and certifying and accrediting agencies for each job title. Web sites that contain useful, current information on the profession, job postings, continuing education programs, and so on are also listed.

Cardiovascular Technologist and Technician

American Society of Echocardiography Professional organization for excellence in cardiovascular ultrasound and its application to patient care. 2100 Gateway Centre Boulevard, Suite 310, Morrisville, North Carolina, 27560, (919) 861-5574 (http://www.asecho.org)

American Registry of Diagnostic Medical Sonography (ARDMS) The primary agency for sonography certification, ARDMS is an independent, nonprofit organization that administers examinations and awards credentials in the areas of diagnostic medical sonography, diagnostic cardiac sonography, vascular interpretation and vascular technology. 51 Monroe Street, Plaza East One, Rockville, Maryland, 20850, (800) 541-9754 (http://www.ardms.org)

Cardiovascular Credentialing International A nonprofit agency offering professional accreditation for cardio techs in five different areas. 1500 Sunday Drive, Suite 102, Raleigh, North Carolina, 27607, (800) 326-0268 (http://www.cci-online.org)

Society for Vascular Ultrasound Credentialing and continuing education for vascular technologists, vascular physicians, vascular lab managers, nurses, and other allied medical ultrasound professionals. 4601 Presidents Drive, Suite 260, Lanham, Maryland, 20706, (301) 459-7550 (http://www.svunet.org)

Certified Nursing Assistant (CNA) and Patient Care Aide

Academy of Certified Health Professionals (ACHP) A nonprofit organization for CNAs dedicated to workforce development, education, and training in health care with a primary focus in geriatrics. ACHP offers well-designed online continuing education courses. 2709 West 13th Street, Joplin, Missouri, 64801, (800) 784-6049 (http://www.achped4u.org)

National Association of Health Care Assistants (NAHCA) A large membership organization providing recognition for outstanding achievements, development training for caregivers, mentoring programs to reduce CNA turnover, and advocacy for issues important to long term care and caregivers. 1201 L Street NW, Washington, DC, 20005, (202) 454-1288 (http://www.nahcacares.org)

Nursing Assistant Central Very helpful Web site with detailed information on training programs for nursing assistants. (http://www.nursingassistantcentral.com)

Dental Hygienist and Dental Assistant

American Dental Association The major professional association for dentists, dental hygienists, and dental assistants. Good information on professional training programs; also a good source of information for patients. 211 East Chicago Avenue, Chicago, Illinois, 60611, (312) 440-2678 (http://www.ada.org)

American Dental Assistants Association (ADAA) The ADAA provides continuing education to dental assistants through home study courses, professional journals and local, state and national meetings with educational agendas. This is the oldest and largest group representing professional dental assistants. 35 East Wacker Drive, Suite 1730, Chicago, Illinois, 60601, (312) 541-1550 (http://www.dentalassistant.org)

American Dental Hygienists' Association (ADHA) The largest professional organization representing the interests of dental hygienists, ADHA offers educational programs and professional support and promotes high standards of professional practice. 444 North Michigan Avenue, Suite 3400, Chicago, Illinois, 60611, (312) 440-8900 (http://www.adha.org)

Commission on Dental Accreditation (CODA) CODA establishes, maintains and applies standards that ensure the quality and continuous improvement of allied dental education programs. Any educational program for dental hygienists or dental assistants should be accredited by CODA. 211 East Chicago Avenue, Chicago, Illinois, 60611, (312) 440-2718 (http://www.ada.org)

Dental Assisting National Board (DANB) A credentialing agency for dental assistants, DANB offers dental assisting exams for certification and recertification. 444 North Michigan Avenue, Suite 900, Chicago, Illinois, 60611, (312) 642-3368 (http://www.danb.org)

Diagnostic Medical Sonographer

American Registry of Diagnostic Medical Sonography (ARDMS) The primary agency for sonography certification, ARDMS has been providing credentialing services since 1975. 51 Monroe Street, Plaza East One, Rockville, Maryland, 20850, (800 541-9754 (http://www.ardms.org)

American Registry of Radiological Technologists (ARRT) The major credentialing organization for radiologic technology workers. ARRT offers certifying exams and continuing education programs. 1255 Northland Drive, St. Paul, Minnesota, 55120, (651) 687-0048 (http://www.arrt.org)

American Society of Echocardiography (ASE) Founded in 1975, ASE is the largest international organization for cardiac imaging. 2100 Gateway Centre Boulevard, Suite 310, Morisville, North Carolina, 27560, (919) 861-5574 (http://www.asecho.org)

Society of Diagnostic Medical Sonography (SDMS) A professional association founded in 1970, SDMS offers continuing educational programs, publishes a scientific journal and newsletter, and sponsors a major national conference each year. 2745 Dallas Parkway, Suite 350, Plano, Texas, 75903 (http://www.sdms.org)

Society for Vascular Ultrasound (SVU) SVU is comprised of more than 4,200 professionals in the field of vascular ultrasound technology. 4601 Presidents Drive, Suite 260, Lanham, Maryland, 30706, (301) 459-7550 (http://www.svunet.org)

Dietitian and Dietetic Technician Registered

American Dietetic Association (ADA) The ADA is the world's largest organization of food and nutrition professionals. Its credentialing agency, the Commission on Dietetic Registration (CDR), offers the national exams for certification as a dietitian or dietetic

technician registered and continuing professional education programs. The ADA's Commission on Accreditation for Dietetics
Education (CADE) accredits training programs. The Web site is
an excellent source of nutrition information for both professionals and patients. 120 South Riverside Plaza, Suite 2000, Chicago,
Illinois, 60606, (800) 877-1600 (http://www.eatright.org)

EMT and Paramedic

**National Association of Emergency Medical Technicians
(NAEMT)** The NAEMT is the only national organization representing the professional interests of all EMS practitioners, including paramedics, emergency medical technicians, first responders,
and other professionals working in pre-hospital emergency medicine, NAEMT provides comprehensive EMS education programs,
including online courses. The Commission on Accreditation of
Educational Programs for the Emergency Medical Services Professions, sponsored by NAEMT, evaluates and accredits educational programs. Box 1400, Clinton, Mississippi, 39060, (800)
34-NAEMT (http://www.naemt.org)

**National Registry of Emergency Medical Technicians
(NREMT)** Founded in 1970 as a result of the recommendations
made by the Committee on Highway Traffic Safety, NREMT is
the national certification agency establishing uniform standards
for training and examination for first responders, basic and intermediate EMTs, and paramedics. 6610 Busch Boulevard, Colum-
bus, Ohio, 43229, (614) 888-4494 (http://www.nremt.org)

Health Educator

American Association for Health Education Professional development for health educators through continuing education,
advocacy, programs, and events. 1900 Association Drive, Reston,
Virginia, 20191, (800) 213-7193 (http://www.aahperd.org)

**The National Commission for Health Education Credentialing,
Inc. (NCHEC)** The primary goal of the NCHEC is to promote professional development, strengthen professional preparation and practice, and certify health education specialists. The organization offers
a national competency-based examination, develops standards for
professional preparation, and promotes professional development
through continuing education. 151 Alta Drive, Suite 303, White-
hall, Pennsylvania, 18052, (888) 624-3248 (http://www.nchec
.org)

Health Information Technician

American Health Information Management Association (AHIMA) The professional organization for health information technicians, AHIMA sets best practices and standards for health information management and offers professional credentialing based on national exams. 233 North Michigan Avenue, 21st Floor, Chicago, Illinois, 60601, (312) 233-1100 (http://www.ahima.org)

Hemodialysis Technician

Board of Nephrology Examiners Nursing and Technology (BONENT) A major international organization for certification of nephrology professionals, BONENT offer credentialing and certification and recertification programs. Over 5,000 nurses and technicians have met BONENT criteria. 901 Pennsylvania Avenue NW, Suite 607, Washington, DC, 20006, (202) 462-1252 (http://www.bonent.org)

Council of Nephrology Nurses and Technicians A professional division of the National Kidney Foundation, the Council offers extensive online continuing education courses for nurses and hemodialysis techs, along with educational meetings and programs and other professional resources. National Kidney Foundation, 30 East 33rd Street, New York, New York, 10016, (800) 622-9010 (http://www.kidney.org)

Nephrology Nursing Certification Commission (NNCC) Established in 1987 to develop and implement certification exams for

Everyone
Knows
Use Up-To-Date Study Materials

All those textbooks, reference books, pocket guides, card decks, and other study materials start to run into a significant expense, both while you are a student and later on as you do your continuing education requirements or work on an advanced degree. It is tempting to buy used materials that can be less costly, but that could end up costing you more in the end. Medicine moves fast, and older material may be outdated even if it is just a couple of years old. Spend the money and stay current.

nephrology nursing, NNCC now also offers certification for clinical hemodialysis technicians. East Holly Avenue, Box 56, Pitman, New Jersey, 08701, (888) 884-NNCC (http://www.nncc-exam.org)

Home Health Aide

Visiting Nurse Associations of America (VNAA) Members of the VNAA are nonprofit visiting nurse agencies (VNAs) and home healthcare and hospice providers, workers who care for and treat approximately four million patients annually. The association supports, promotes and advances the nation's network of VNAs through advocacy, education and collaboration and by providing with products, resources, continuing education programs, and the support they need. 900 19th Street NW, Suite 200, Washington, DC, 20006, (202) 384-1420 (http://www.vnaa.org)

Laboratory Technologist and Technician

American Association of Blood Banks (AABB) AABB is an international association representing individuals and institutions involved in activities related to transfusion and cellular therapies, including transplantation medicine. AABB member facilities are responsible for collecting virtually all of the nation's blood supply and transfusing more than 80 percent of all blood and blood components used in the United States. The association offers certification for blood bank technicians and phlebotomists, continuing education programs, and a good directory of training programs. 8101 Glenbrook Road, Bethesda, Maryland, 20814, (301) 907-6977 (http://www.aabb.org)

American Medical Technologists (AMT) The American Medical Technologists (AMT) is a nonprofit certification agency and professional membership association representing over 41,000 individuals in allied health care. Certifications are offered for medical technologists, medical laboratory technicians, medical lab assistants, medical assistants, medical administrative specialists, phlebotomy technicians, dental assistants, allied health instructors, and clinical laboratory consultants. 10700 West Higgins, Suite 150, Rosemont, Illinois, 60018, (800) 275-1268 (http://www.amt1.com)

American Association of Bioanalysts (AAB) A national professional association whose members include medical technologists, medical laboratory technicians, physician office laboratory technicians, and phlebotomists, AAB offers national certification in these fields through the AAB Board of Registry (ABOR). 906

Olive Street, Suite 1200, St. Louis, Missouri, 63101, (314) 241-1445 (http://www.aab.org)

American Society for Clinical Pathology (ASCP) Certification by the ASCP Board of Registry (BOR)/Board of Certification (BOC) has been the industry standard for laboratory professionals since 1928. Over 430,000 individuals have been certified by the BOC; certifications are offered in 20 different categories. ASCP also offers an extensive range of continuing medical laboratory education programs. 33 West Monroe Street, Suite 1600, Chicago, Illinois, 60603, (800) 267-2727 (http://www.ascp.org)

National Accrediting Agency for Clinical Laboratory Sciences Accredited programs from this agency include clinical laboratory scientist, medical technologist, clinical laboratory technician, medical laboratory technician, cytogenetic technologist, diagnostic molecular scientist, histologic technician, histotechnologist, and pathologists' assistant. The Web site has a good search tool for finding accredited training programs. 5600 North River Road, Suite 720, Rosemont, Illinois, 60018, (773) 714-8880 (http://www.naacls.org)

National Phlebotomy Association Founded in 1978, the National Phlebotomy Association is the only organization concerned with all aspects of educating and certifying phlebotomists. The association helps develop educational programs, provides accreditation for individuals, and offers continuing education programs. The NPA has certified over 15,000 phlebotomists and 75 accredited teaching programs. 1901 Brightseat Road, Landover, Maryland, 20785, (301) 386-4200 (http://www.nationalphlebotomy.org)

Licensed Practical Nurse/Licensed Vocational Nurse

National Federation of Licensed Practical Nurses (NFLPN) The professional organization for licensed practical nurses and licensed vocational nurses and practical/vocational nursing students in the United States, NFLPN promotes continued competence with education and certification programs. The Web site also offers a valuable career center. 600 Poole Drive, Garner, North Carolina, 27529, (919) 779-0046 (http://www.nflpn.org)

Medical Assistant

American Association of Medical Assistants (AAMA) Founded in 1955, the AAMA is devoted exclusively to the medical assisting profession. The association works to facilitate CAAHEP

On the Cutting Edge

Online Reference Sources

Today one of the most important tools for any health care professional is a personal digital assistant, or PDA, such as a Blackberry or iPhone. These handy electronic devices help you keep track of your shifts and hours and let you make notes to yourself about patients. They are also a very convenient, fast way to access online standard medical reference materials such as drug lists, medical dictionaries, anatomy guides, information about medical tests, and much more. Of course, this information is also available in bulky, expensive books. The online versions are not only much more accessible, they are constantly updated so you know the information is current. Many professional sites charge an annual fee for access; your employer may have site licenses that let you sign on at no charge.

accreditation of medical assisting programs. Graduates from accredited medical assisting programs are eligible to take the CMA (AAMA) certification examination. In addition, AAMA offers recertification. Local chapters and state societies sponsor seminars and workshops; on the national level, AAMA offers a professional journal, continuing education articles, convention workshops, and self-study courses. 20 North Wacker Drive, Suite 1575, Chicago, Illinois, 60606, (800) 228-2262 (http://www.aama-ntl.org)

American Medical Technologists (AMT) Established in 1939, AMT provides many personal and professional services to aid its members in developing their careers. 10700 West Higgins, Suite 150, Rosemont, Illinois, 68108, (800) 275-1268 (http://www.amt1.com)

Medical Coder

American Academy of Professional Coders (AAPC) The primary professional association for medical coders. AAPC provides certified credentials to some 82,000 medical coders in physician offices, hospital outpatient facilities, ambulatory surgical centers and in payer organizations. CPC, CPC-H, CPC-P, and CIRCC are the gold standard certification for medical coding. 2480 South 3850 West, Suite B, Salt Lake City, Utah, 84120, (800) 626-CODE (http://www.aapc.com)

Medical Transcriptionist
Association for Healthcare Documentation Integrity (AHDI) Formerly known the American Association for Medical Transcription, the Association for Healthcare Documentation Integrity (AHDI) is the world's largest professional society representing the clinical documentation sector. AHDI offers certification exams to become a certified medical transcriptionist (CMT). The association also advocates for the profession and for high standards in medical transcription. 4230 Kiernan Avenue, Suite 130, Modesto, California, 95356, (800) 982-2182 (http://www.ahdionline.org)

Nuclear Medicine Technologist
American Registry of Radiologic Technologists (ARRT) Founded in 1922, ARRT now represents almost 300,000 registered technologists. 1225 Northland Drive, St. Paul, Minnesota, 55210, (651) 687-0048 (http://www.arrt.org)

Joint Review Committee on Educational Programs in Nuclear Medicine Technology (JRCNMT) The nationally recognized accrediting agency for educational programs for nuclear medicine technologists. 2000 West Danforth Road, Suite 130, Edmond, Oklahoma, 73003, (405) 285-0546 (http://www.jrcnmt.org)

Nuclear Medicine Technology Certification Board (NMTCB) The Nuclear Medicine Technology Certification Board creates and administers certification exams for nuclear medicine technologists (NMTs). The organization also offers specialty exams for NMTs in nuclear cardiology, radiographers, and radiation therapists in positron emission tomography (the PET exam). 3558 Habersham at Northlake, Building I, Tucker, Georgia, 30084, (404) 315-1739 (http://www.nmtcb.org)

Nurse Anesthetist
American Association of Nurse Anesthetists (AANA) Founded in 1931, the AANA is the professional organization for more than 90 percent of the nation's certified registered nurse anesthetists. The National Board on Certification and Recertification of Nurse Anesthetists (NBCRNA), a division of AANA, manages the certification programs. Another division, Council on Accreditation of

Nurse Anesthesia Educational Programs (COA), accredits training programs. 222 South Prospect Avenue, Park Ridge, Illinois, 60068, (847) 692-7050 (http://www.aana.com)

Nurse Midwife

American College of Nurse-Midwives (ACNM) Dating back to 1929, the American College of Nurse-Midwives (ACNM) is the oldest women's health care organization in the United States. ACNM represents the interests of certified nurse-midwives and certified midwives through research, continuing education programs, establishing clinical practice standards, and advocating with state and federal agencies and members of Congress. The Accreditation Commission for Midwifery Education (ACME) is the national accrediting agency for nurse-midwifery education programs. 8403 Colesville Road, Suite 1550, Silver Spring, Maryland, 20910, (240) 485-1800 (http://www.midwife.org)

American Nurses Credentialing Center This subsidary of the American Nurses Credentialing Center offers members internationally recognized credentialing programs in many specialty practice areas. 8515 Georgia Avenue, Suite 400, Silver Spring, Maryland, 20910, (800) 284-2378. (http://nursecredentialing.org)

Association of Women's Health, Obstetric and Neonatal Nurses (AWHONN) The goal of AWHONN is to improve and promote the health of women and newborns and to strengthen the nursing profession through the delivery of superior advocacy, research, education and other professional and clinical resources to nurses and other health care professionals. The Web site is an excellent source for information about continuing education, professional issues, and patient information. 2000 L Street NW, Suite 740, Washington, DC, 20036, (800) 673-8499 (http://www.awhonn.org)

Nurse Practitioner

American Academy of Nurse Practitioners (AANP) As the largest and only full-service national professional membership organization for NPs of all specialties, AANP represents the interests of the more than 125,000 NPs currently practicing in the United States and continually advocates at local, state, and federal levels for the recognition of NPs as providers of high-quality, cost-effective, and personalized healthcare. Box 12846, Austin, Texas, 78711, (512) 442-4262 (http://www.aanp.org)

Occupational Therapist and Occupational Therapy Assistant

American Occupational Therapy Association (AOTA) Established in 1917, AOTA is the national professional association representing the interests and concerns of occupational therapy practitioners. AOTA's 39,000 members include occupational therapists, occupational therapy assistants, and occupational therapy students. The Accreditation Council for Occupational Therapy Education (ACOTE) is the accrediting agency for training programs in occupational therapy. 4720 Montgomery Lane, Bethesda, Maryland, 20824, (301) 652-2682 (http://www.aota.org)

National Board for Certification in Occupational Therapy (NBCOT) A not-for-profit credentialing agency, NBCOT provides certification for the occupational therapy profession as an occupational therapist registered (OTR) or certified occupational therapy assistants (COTA). 12 South Summit Avenue, Suite 100, Gaithersburg, Maryland, 20877, (301) 990-7979 (http://www.nbcot.org)

Pharmacy Technician

American Association of Pharmacy Technicians (AAPT) AAPT promotes the role of technicians in the safe and cost-effective dispensing and use of medications and provides continuing education programs and services to help technicians update their skills to keep pace with changes in pharmacy services. The Web site has an excellent job search tool. Box 1447, Greensboro, North Carolina, 27402, (877) 368-4771 (http://www.pharmacytechnician.com)

Pharmacy Technician Certification Board (PTCB) Starting in 1995, the PTCB has developed and administered a nationally recognized and accredited certification exam for pharmacy technicians. Individuals who meet all eligibility requirements and who successfully pass the national Pharmacy Technician Certification Examination may use the designation CPhT after their name. 2215 Constitution Avenue NW, Washington, DC, 20037, (800) 363-8012 (http://www.ptcb.org)

Physical Therapist and Physical Therapy Assistant

American Physical Therapy Association (APTA) The American Physical Therapy Association (APTA) is a national professional organization representing more than 72,000 members. Its goal is to foster advancements in physical therapy practice, research, and education. The Web site is an excellent source of professional and patient information. APTA is the parent organization for the Commission on Accreditation in Physical Therapy Education, which reviews and accredits physical therapy training programs. 1111 North Fairfax Street, Alexandria, Virginia, 22314, (800) 999-2782 (http://www.apta.org)

Federation of State Boards of Physical Therapy The Federation of State Boards of Physical Therapy develops and administers the National Physical Therapy Examination (NPTE) for both physical therapists and physical therapist assistants in 53 jurisdictions: the 50 states, the District of Columbia, Puerto Rico, and the Virgin Islands. These high-stakes exams assess the basic entry-level competence for first time licensure or registration as a PT or PTA. 511 Wythe Street, Alexandria, Virginia, 22314, (703) 684-8406 (http://www.fsbpt.org)

Physician Assistant

American Academy of Physician Assistants (AAPA) This is the only national professional association that represents all PAs across all medical and surgical specialties in all 50 states, the District of Columbia, Guam, the armed forces, and the federal services. AAPA provides comprehensive support and advocacy for the 73,000 physician assistants in practice today. 950 North Washington Street, Alexandria, Virginia, 22314, (703) 836-2272 (http://www.aapa.org)

National Commission on Certification of Physician Assistants (NCCPA) The only credentialing organization for physician assistants in the United States. Approximately 60,000 physician assistants have been certified by NCCPA. To attain certification, PAs must graduate from an accredited PA program and pass the Physician Assistant National Certifying Exam (PANCE). 12000 Findley Road, Suite 200, Duluth, Georgia, 30097, (678) 417-8100 (http://www.nccpa.net)

Radiation Therapy Technologist

American Registry of Radiologic Technologists (ARRT) ARRT offers certifying exams and continuing education programs. 1255 Northland Drive, St. Paul, Minnesota, 55120 (650) 687-0048 (http://arrt.org)

American Society of Radiologic Technicians (ASRT) The major professional association for registered radiologic technologists, ASRT is the world's largest radiologic science organization with more 120,000 members. ASRT provides its members with educational opportunities, promotes radiologic technology as a career, and monitors state and federal legislation that affects the profession. The ASRT publishes two peer-reviewed research journals and a monthly newsmagazine. 15000 Central Avenue SE, Albuquerque, New Mexico, 87123, (800) 444-2778 (http://www.asrt.org)

Joint Review Committee on Education in Radiologic Technology The official accrediting agency for traditional and distance delivery educational programs in radiography, radiation therapy, magnetic resonance, and medical dosimetry. 20 North Wacker Drive, Suite 2850, Chicago, Illinois, 60606, (312) 704-5300 (http://www.jrcert.org)

Registered Nurse

American Assembly for Men in Nursing A professional organization for male nurses that encourages the participation of men in nursing and provides support to those already in the profession. 6700 Oporto-Madrid Boulevard, Birmingham, Alabama, 35206, (205) 956-0146 (http://www.aamn.org)

American Association of Critical-Care Nurses The largest specialty nursing organization in the world, representing the interests of more than 500,000 nurses who are charged with the responsibility of caring for acutely and critically ill patients. The association offers seven different certification programs. 101 Columbia, Aliso Viejo, California, 92656, (800) 899-AACN (http://www.aacn.org)

American Board of Nursing Specialties (ABNS) ABNS is a not-for-profit, membership that promotes specialty nursing certification. ABNS member organizations represent more than a half million certified registered nurses worldwide. The Accreditation Board for Specialty Nursing Certification (ABSNC), formerly the ABNS Accreditation Council, is the only accrediting body specifically for nursing certification—this is the program that certifies other certification programs in nursing. 610 Thornhill Lane, Aurora, Ohio, 44202, (330) 995-9172 (http://www.nursingcertification.org)

American Nurses Association (ANA) The American Nurses Association (ANA) is the only full-service professional organization representing the interests of the nation's 2.9 million registered nurses. Excellent source of information for anyone interested in nursing as a career and those already in the profession. The Nurses Career Center on the Web site is a good place to look for a job;

the continuing education area has solid information. A subsidiary, the American Nurses Credentialing Center (ANCC), offers certification in a number of nursing specialties and certifies the Magnet Recognition Program for outstanding hospitals. *American Nurse Today,* the official journal of the ANA, reaches over 175,000 dedicated nurses; the Web site at http://www.americannursetoday.com is an additional source of information on continuing education and nursing practice. 8515 Georgia Avenue, Silver Spring, Maryland, 20910, (800) 274-4ANA (http://www.ana.org)

Discover Nursing A Web site, sponsored by Johnson & Johnson, encouraging individuals to enter the nursing field. Excellent information for those thinking about nursing and related areas as a career. http://www.discovernursing.com)

MinorityNurse.com A career and education resource for minority nursing students and professionals. The Web site has outstanding database tools for finding scholarships, nursing schools, and jobs. (http://www.minoritynurse.com)

National Association of Clinical Nurse Specialists (NACNS) Found in 1995, NACNS promotes the unique, high-value contribution of the clinical nurse specialist to the health and well-being of individuals, families, groups, and communities. The association promotes and advances the practice of nursing. Good source of information about training programs and job listings. 2090 Linglestown Road, Suite 107, Harrisburg, Pennsylvania, 17110, (717) 234-6799 (http://www.nacns.org)

National Council of State Boards of Nursing This nonprofit organization develops the major nursing exams, including the NCLEX-RN, NCLEX-PN, NNAAP, and MACE. It also sponsors the Nurse Licensure Compact, which allows nurses licensed in one participating state to work in others without needing to be re-licensed. The Web site is a crucial source of information about the nursing exams and NLC. 111 East Wacker Drive, Chicago, Illinois, 60601, (312) 525-3600 (http://www.ncsbn.org)

National Gerontological Nursing Association (NGNA) Members of NGNA are dedicated to the care of older adults across diverse care settings. The association sponsors certification as a gerontological nurse, clinical nurse specialist gerontology, and gerontological nurse practitioner. 7794 Grow Drive, Pensacola, Florida, 32514, (800) 723-0560 (http://www.ngna.org)

National Student Nurses Association With a membership of approximately 50,000 nationwide, the National Student Nurses'

Association mentors the professional development of future nurses and facilitates their entrance into the profession by providing educational resources, leadership opportunities, and career guidance. Sponsors a major national conference each year. 45 Main Street, Suite 606, Brooklyn, New York, 11201, (718) 210-0705 (http://www.nsna.org)

NCLEX Examination Program, Pearson Professional Testing Students planning to take the NCLEX or related health care certification exams must register through this Web site. Details of the exams and the testing procedures are found here. 5601 Green Valley Drive, Bloomington, Minnesota, 55437, (866) 496-2539 (http://www.vue.com)

NurseConnect An online nursing community and networking site for nurses and other healthcare professionals. Excellent starting point for career guidance and job searching. 12400 High Bluff Drive, San Diego, California, 92130, (877) 585-4535 (http://www.nurseconnect.com)

NurseZone An online community dedicated to providing student nurses, new nurses, and experienced nurses with professional and personal development information and opportunities. Lots of

Everyone Knows

Using PubMed

PubMed at http://www.pubmed.gov is an integrated online search and retrieval system for biomedical literature—it provides free access to abstracts and often also to full articles from thousands of medical journals. PubMed is part of the National Center for Biotechnology Information (NCBI) at the National Library of Medicine (NLM), located at the U.S. National Institutes of Health (NIH). It is the starting point for any sort of biomedical research project. The NCBI Web site also includes Bookshelf, a large and growing collection of online medical books, including many that are designed for allied health professionals and consumers. Using PubMed is easy once you get the hang of it—if you are new to the system, start with the tutorial.

helpful content, community forums and blogs, good links to continuing education courses, jobs and a variety of nursing-related Web sites. 12400 High Bluff Drive, San Diego, California, 92130, (877) 585-4535 (http://www.nursezone.com)

Respiratory Therapist and Respiratory Therapy Aide

American Association for Respiratory Care (AARC) The leading national and international professional association for respiratory care, with more than 47,000 members worldwide. The Web site has a good career resources section and links to education programs. 11030 Ables Lane, Dallas, Texas, 75229, (972) 243-2272 (http://www.aarc.org)

Committee on Accreditation for Respiratory Care (CoARC) The official accrediting agency for respiratory care training programs. 1248 Harwood Road, Bedford, Texas, 76021, (817) 283-2835 (http://www.coarc.com)

National Board for Respiratory Care (NBRC) NBRC develops and administers the credentialing exams for respiratory care professionals. 8310 Nieman Road, Lenexa, Kansas, 66214, (913) 599-4200 (http://www.nbrc.org)

Speech-Language Pathologist and Audiologist

American Speech-Language-Hearing Association (ASHA) The professional, scientific, and credentialing association for speech-language pathologists and audiologists. The Web site has good information for students, professionals, and the public. A subsidiary, the Council on Academic Accreditation in Audiology and Speech-Language Pathology, develops and administers the credentialing exams. 10801 Rockville Pike, Rockville, Maryland, 20852, (800) 638-8255 (http://www.asha.org)

Surgical Technologist

Association of Surgical Assistants and Association of Surgical Technologists The only national professional associations for surgical assistants and technologists, ASA and AST offer numerous services to members. The associations sponsor the Accreditation Review Committee on Education in Surgical Technology (ARC-ST), which accredits training programs, and the National Board of Surgical Technology and Surgical Assisting (NBSTSA), which develops and administers certification exams. 6 West Dry

Creek Circle, Suite 100, Littleton, Colorado, 80120, (800) 707-0057 (http://www.surgicalassistant.org) (http://www.ast.org)

Books and Periodicals

Books

In this section we list a selection of classic and current books about being a health care professional—memoirs, biographies, and narratives. We also list some important books on the health care workplace, the experience of illness, and other topics that will give you a broader picture of medicine and health care. We have tried to select titles that are also well written and engaging so that your leisure reading will not feel like work.

Emergency Medicine
Ambulance Girl: How I Saved Myself by Becoming an EMT. By Jane Stern (Three Rivers Press, 2004). How helping others helps you.
The Blood of Strangers: Stories from Emergency Medicine. By Frank Huyler (Picador, 2004). The life and death realities of the emergency room, told by an ER doctor.
Blood, Sweat, and Tea: Real-Life Adventures in an Inner-City Ambulance. By Tom Reynolds (Andrews McMeel, 2008). An EMT in London—where things are not very different from any American city.
Confessions of Emergency Room Doctors. By Rocky Land (Andrews McMeel, 2007). More than 200 ER docs share their favorite war stories.
Emergency Doctor. By Edward Ziegler (HarperCollins, 2004). At New York City's Bellevue Hospital, no one is turned away—tales from one of the oldest, busiest, and best ERs in the country.
Emergency! True Stories from the Nation's ERs. By Mark Brown (St. Martin's 1997). Life and death from ERs across the country.
Just Here Trying to Save a Few Lives: Tales of Life and Death from the ER. By Pamela Grim (Grand Central Publishing, 2002). The adrenaline-fueled chaos of an urban ER, from a doctor's perspective.
The Knife and Gun Club: Scenes from an Emergency Room. By Eugene Richards (Atlantic Monthly Press, 1995). An uncensored look at what goes on in one of the nation's top trauma centers.
Paramedic: On the Front Lines of Medicine. By Peter Canning (Ivy Books, 1998). From waiting around to racing against time, from

minor mishaps to life-threatening accidents—typical days in the life of a paramedic.

Rescue 471: A Paramedic's Stories. By Peter Canning (Ballantine Books, 2000). Stabilize, load, and go—what a paramedic unit really does.

Something for the Pain: One Doctor's Account of Life and Death in the ER. By Paul Austin. (Norton, 2008). Beautifully written ER tales from a firefighter turned emergency medicine doctor.

Talking Trauma. By Timothy Tangherlini (University Press of Mississippi, 1998). The stories paramedics tell only each other.

Trauma Junkie: Memoirs of an Emergency Flight Nurse. By Janice Hudson (Firefly Books, 2001). Dramatic rescues of critically injured patients.

The Experience of Illness

The Anatomy of Hope: How People Prevail in the Face of Illness. By Jerome Groopman (Random House, 2005). The vital role of hope in overcoming illness.

The Body Broken: A Memoir. By Lynne Greenberg (Random House, 2009). Dealing with chronic pain and medical misdiagnosis.

Dancing at the River's Edge: A Patient and Her Doctor Negotiate Life with Chronic Illness. By Alida Brill (Schaffner Press, 2009). Living with lupus and coping with the health system.

How We Die: Reflections on Life's Final Chapter. By Sherwin B. Nuland (Vintage, 1995). The reality and meaning of death; sensitive but not sentimental.

The Lonely Patient: How We Experience Illness. By Michael Stein (Harper Perennial, 2008). The emotional toll of serious illness and disability, for the patient, the family, and the caregivers.

The Man Who Mistook His Wife for a Hat. By Oliver Sachs (Touchstonc, 1998). The classic work on neurological diseases and loss of function; beautifully written.

The Spirit Catches You and You Fall Down. By Anne Fadiman (Farrar, Straus and Giroux, 1998). The tragic consequences of cultural differences in understanding epilepsy.

Fiction and Literature

Arrowsmith. By Sinclair Lewis (Signet Classics, 1925). The classic novel about a dedicated doctor—the inspiration for countless careers in medicine.

The House of God: The Classic Novel of Life and Death in an American Hospital. By Samuel Shem (Dell, 2003). What it is really like to be an intern in a busy urban hospital, from the absurd to the inspirational.

A Life in Medicine: A Literary Anthology. By Robert Coles (New Press, 2002). Short essays, poems, stories, and memoirs reflecting the human side of medicine.

History of Medicine and Medical Classics

The Alarming History of Medicine: Amusing Anecdotes from Hippocrates to Heart Transplants. By Richard Gordon (St. Martin's Press, 1993). A skeptic's view of the history of medicine—what doctors do not want you to know.

The Discovery of Insulin. By Michael Bliss (University of Chicago Press, 2007). How diabetes was conquered. Medical history that reads like a novel.

Everyone Knows

Professional Journals

Keeping up with new developments in your field is important for professional success. As part of your membership in a professional association, you will probably get a subscription to a professional journal or magazine and perhaps a newsletter that will help you keep up to date. You will also probably get member access to an informative Web site that includes job listings and online job fairs. For most allied health careers, another excellent source of information is Advanceweb.com, a company that produces print and online magazines and helpful Web sites, with job postings and much more. Subscriptions and Web access are free for practitioners. For information:

Advanceweb.com
2900 Horizon Drive
King of Prussia, PA 19406
(800) 355-5627
http://www.advanceweb.com

Doctors: The Biography of Medicine. By Sherwin B. Nuland (Vintage, 1995). The history of medicine told through the lives of pioneering practitioners.

The Greatest Benefit to Mankind: A Medical History of Humanity. By Roy Porter (Norton, 1999). Readable, anecdotal history of medicine.

The Medical Detectives. By Berton Roueche (Plume, 1991). On the trail of medical mysteries.

Microbe Hunters. By Paul de Kruif (Harvest, 2002). The classic description of the pioneering work of Pasteur, Koch, and other giants of microbiology. First published in 1960 and still a great read.

The Mold in Dr. Florey's Coat: The Story of the Penicillin Miracle. By Eric Lax (Owl Books, 2005). The discovery and development of penicillin during World War II.

Notes on Nursing: What It Is and What It Is Not. By Florence Nightingale (reprint edition, BiblioLife, 2009). No-nonsense, scientific nursing by the woman who invented it. A must read for any nursing student.

Plagues and Peoples. By William H. McNeill (Anchor, 1977). The role of epidemic disease in human history. An outstanding and very readable work of scholarship.

Rats, Lice, and History. By Hans Zinsser (reprint edition, Transaction Publishers, 2007). How the Black Plague and other epidemics transformed society.

The Social Transformation of American Medicine. By Paul Starr (Basic Books, 1984). Landmark history of how the American health care system has evolved; Pulitzer Prize winner in 1983.

The True Story of Mary Benjamin, R.N. By Peggy Anderson (Berkley, 2007). Eight weeks in the daily life of a dedicated nurse at a large city hospital.

Hospital Life

Becoming a Doctor: A Journey of Initiation in Medical School. By Melvin Konner (Penguin, 1988). An anthropologist goes to medical school. Revealing, highly critical look at medical training.

Burn Unit: Saving Lives after the Flames. By Barbara Ravage (Da Capo, 2005). Brilliantly written look at life on the burn unit, one of the most demanding areas of medicine.

First, Do No Harm. By Lisa Belkin (Fawcett, 1994). Medical ethics and critical care decisions, as seen through cases at a Houston hospital.

Hospital: Man, Woman, Birth, Death, Infinity, Plus Red Tape, Bad Behavior, Money, God and Diversity on Steroids. By Julie Salamon (Penguin, 2008). An in-depth, honest look at a busy urban hospital in Brooklyn, from top to bottom.

Intensive Care: A Doctor's Journal. By John F. Murray (University of California Press, 2002). Twenty-eight days of daily rounds in an intensive care unit: how doctors and nurses make their decisions.

A Not Entirely Benign Procedure: Four Years as a Medical Student. By Perry Klass (Plume, 1994). Learning to be a doctor from the perspective of a woman and mother.

On Call: A Doctor's Days and Nights in Residency. By Emily R. Transue (St. Martin's Press, 2005). A young doctor's journal of the ups and downs during her three-year residency. Vivid depiction of the realities and limits of medicine.

OR: The True Story of 24 Hours in a Hospital Operating Room. By B.D. Colen (Signet, 1994). Six weeks of emergency surgery cases at a major teaching hospital—the split-second decisions, the life-saving surgeons, the sometimes tragic outcomes.

Midwives

Baby Catcher: Chronicles of a Modern Midwife. By Peggy Vincent. (Scribner, 2003). From obstetrics nurse in a hospital to a midwife for home births.

The Blue Cotton Gown: A Midwife's Memoirs. By Patricia Harman (Beacon Press, 2008). An inside look at the daily life of a midwife in a struggling women's health clinic.

Nursing

American Nightingale: The Story of Frances Slanger, Forgotten Heroine of Normandy. By Bob Welch (Atria, 2005). The remarkable story of an ordinary nurse in World War II who courageously went ashore with the first soldiers at the Normandy invasion and was killed when her hospital was shelled.

And If I Perish: Frontline US Army Nurses in World War II. By Evelyn Monahan (Anchor, 2004). A valuable account of the often-forgotten contributions of nurses under fire.

Condition Critical. By Echo Heron (Ivy Books, 1995). A personal memoir of tending the sickest of the sick.

Cooked: An Inner City Nursing Memoir. By Carol Karels (Arcania, 2005). How the nurses hold it all together at a chaotic inner-city hospital.

Home Before Morning: The Story of an Army Nurse in Vietnam. By Lynda Van Devanter (University of Massachusetts Press, 2001). The human cost of war comes across vividly in this memoir by an Army nurse who served at an evacuation hospital in Vietnam.

Intensive Care: The Story of a Nurse. By Echo Heron (Ivy Books, 1988). Lessons learned from ten years of treating intensive care patients.

Life Support: Three Nurses on the Front Lines. By Suzanne Gordon (ILR Press, 2007). Follow three outspoken nurses on their rounds each day.

The Making of a Nurse. By Tilda Shalof (McClelland & Stewart, 2008). Unflinchingly honest and often funny stories of a new nurse finding her way.

Nurses. By Michael Brown (Ivy Books, 1992). The daily ups and downs of nursing based on real-life experience, from students to seasoned veterans.

A Nurse's Story. By Tilda Shalof (McClelland & Stewart, 2005). An insightful look into the real world of nursing, especially in the intensive care unit.

Tending Lives: Nurses on the Medical Front. By Echo Heron (Ivy Books, 1999). Oral histories from experienced nurses; great stories give a realistic picture of nursing.

We Band of Angels: The Untold Story of American Nurses Trapped on Bataan by the Japanese. By Elizabeth Norman (Atria, 2000). Nurses acting far above the call of duty under appalling conditions during World War II.

Woman of Valor: Clara Barton and the Civil War. By Stephen P. Oates (Free Press, 1994). Inspiring biography of the founder of the American Red Cross.

Surgery

Better: A Surgeon's Notes on Performance. By Atul Gawande (Picador, 2008). A thoughtful, very well-written discussion of how health care professionals learn from mistakes.

Complications: A Surgeon's Notes on an Imperfect Science. By Atul Gawande (Picador, 2003). The myth of medical infallibility is demolished in this honest look at the practice of medicine.

Final Exam: A Surgeon's Reflections on Mortality. By Pauline W. Chen (Vintage, 2008). A critique of end-of-life care from a deeply compassionate transplant surgeon.

Gifted Hands: The Ben Carson Story. By Ben Carson (Zondervan, 1996). Overcoming prejudice and a disadvantaged background to become a leading neurosurgeon.

Hot Lights, Cold Steel: Life, Death, and Sleepless Nights in a Surgeon's First Years. By Michael J. Collins (St. Martin's Press, 2006). The making of a young surgeon, medical mistakes and all.

The Surgeons: Life and Death in a Top Heart Center. By Charles Morris (Norton, 2008). A journalist reports on six months in the elite cardiac surgery center at Columbia-Presbyterian hospital in New York City.

When the Air Hits Your Brain: Tales from Neurosurgery. By Frank Vertosick (Norton, 2008). From naive young intern to world-class neurosurgeon.

Thinking about Medicine

Dissecting Death: Secrets of a Medical Examiner. By Frederick Zugibe (Broadway, 2006). Ten challenging cases and their solutions, from a veteran forensic pathologist.

How Doctors Think. By Jerome Groopman (Mariner Books, 2008). An insightful look at medical reasoning and why doctors usually get it right but sometimes get it wrong.

How Not to Die: Surprising Lessons on Living Longer, Safer and Healthier from America's Favorite Medical Examiner. By Jan Garavaglia (Three Rivers Press, 2009). Dr. G of television fame discusses her most fascinating cases.

How We Live. By Sherwin B. Nuland (Vintage, 1998). A very accessible look at the various body systems and what can go wrong, from a surgeon's perspective.

Second Opinions: Stories of Intuition and Choice in the Changing World of Medicine. By Jerome Groopman (Penguin, 2001). Decision-making in medicine, based on a eight clinical studies.

The Soul of Medicine. By Sherwin B. Nuland (Kaplan Publishing, 2009). A dozen famed specialists describe their most memorable patients.

Unnatural Death: Confessions of a Medical Examiner. By Michael M. Baden (Ballantine, 1990). Famous cases from a long-time New York City forensic pathologist.

Periodicals

Advance for Nurses This periodical, free to qualified nursing professionals, is an excellent compendium of news, commentary, technological advancements, and professional development trends throughout the industry. (http://nursing.advanceweb.com)

American Journal of Nursing Established in 1900, AJN is an award-winning, peer-reviewed, monthly journal publishing a broad range of articles., Issues include news analysis, commentary and presentation of original research. (http://journals.lww.com/ajnonline/pages/default.aspx)

Critical Care Nurse This bimonthly periodical covers the latest advances in critical care, including the newest clinical techniques, information on critical care, pharmacology, nutrition, pulmonary care, and neurology. (http://ccn.aacnjournals.org)

Nursing The standard periodical for those involved in any branch of the nursing field specializes in up-to-date information on drugs, diseases, nursing care strategies, and ethical and legal issues. (http://www.nursing2010.com)

Professional Case Management This journal features best practices and industry standards for professional case managers, including information on coordination of patient care, efficient use of resources, and ways to improve quality of care. (http://journals.lww.com/professionalcasemanagementjournal/pages/defautl/aspx)

Web Sites

This section lists useful Web sites for health care workers in two crucial areas: career development and general medical and clinical information.

Career Development

These Web sites are excellent starting points for learning more about careers in different areas of health care and for advancing your career in your chosen field. They are also a good place to begin your hunt for the job that will take you to the next level.

Absolutely Health Care Primarily a job hunting site; also offers good education resources and licensing information. (http://www.healthjobsusa.com)

Advance for Health Care Jobs Extensive job postings and a good search engine for job fairs. (http://health-care-jobs.advanceweb.com)

AllHealthCare.com News, education resources, career guides, job search, career networking, mentorship; part of Monster Worldwide. (http://www.allhealthcare.com)

American Medical Association Health Care Careers The online Health Care Careers Directory. This site contains information about 81 careers in health care and more than 8,000 accredited educational programs. (http://www.ama-assn.org))

Career Voyages A collaboration between the U.S. Department of Labor and the U.S. Department of Education; the health care section has solid information on the skills and education needed for a wide range of jobs. (http://www.careervoyages.gov)

DiscoverNursing.com Sponsored by Johnson & Johnson, this is an outstanding site for those considering a career in nursing. Excellent videos. (http://www.discovernursing.com)

DiversityAlliedHealth.com A career and education resource for minority nursing professional, students, and faculty. (http://www.DiversityAlliedHealth.com)

ExploreHealthCareers.org) Comprehensive source of accurate, up-to-date information about the health professions; information on and links to health-related education/training programs. (http://www.explorehealthcareers.org))

Health Career Web Large heath care professional job site that also offers social networking. (http://www.healthcareerweb.com)

Health Professions Network Comprehensive list of health care professions, with detailed descriptions and analysis of job opportunities. (http://www.healthpronet.org))

Nurse.com Nursing news, nursing jobs, nursing continuing education, free online magazine, and more. (http://www.nurse.com)

Therapy Times Community Web site providing resources for music, nursing, nutrition, occupational, pediatric, physical, respiratory and speech therapists to improve patient care and further their careers. Sponsored by magazine/newsletter publisher Therapy Times. (http://www.therapytimes.com)

General Medical and Clinical Information

Keeping up with developments in your field is crucial to success. In addition to regularly reading the newsletters, journals, and other publications put out by the professional organizations in your field, it is important to keep up with developments both in your area and in health care overall. This section lists reliable, up-to-date Web sites that are excellent sources of overall information about medical conditions and current developments.

Alternative Medicine Foundation Providing consumers and professionals with responsible information on the integration of alternative and conventional medicine. (http://www.Amfoundation.org))

American College of Cardiology (ACC) The ACC advocates for quality cardiovascular care through education, research promotion, development and application of standards and guidelines. (http://www.acc.org))

American Heart Association (AHA) Definitive source for scientific statements, practice guidelines and clinical updates on cardiovascular disease and stroke. Excellent source for patient information as well. (http://www.americanheart.org))

American Medical Association (AMA) Oriented primarily to physicians and medical students, but also a good source of information on careers in health care and current issues in medicine. (http://www.ama-assn.org)

Cardiosource Comprehensive and very current information about cardiology; includes summaries of recent journal articles, expert opinions, case studies, and continuing medical education options. Sponsored by American College of Cardiology. (http://www.cardiosource.com)

Centers for Disease Control and Prevention (CDC) Excellent, unbiased source of health information for consumers and professionals. Includes latest treatment guidelines and resources for many diseases and conditions. (http://www.cdc.gov)

Clinical Care Options Interactive resources and medical education programs for health care professionals, particularly in oncology, liver disease, and HIV/AIDS. (http://www.clinicaloptions.com)

eMedicine.com Clinical reference for health care professionals; thousands of up-to-date articles in medicine, surgery, and pediatrics. The professional side of the popular consumer medicine Web site WebMD.com. (http://www.emedicine.com)

Healthfinder The starting point for finding health care information on government Web sites such as the National Institutes of Health. (http://www.healthfinder.gov)

Herb Research Foundation Reliable source of accurate, science-based information on the health beneifts and safety of herbal remedies. (http://www.herbs.org)

Institute of Medicine (IOM) The IOM serves as adviser to the nation to improve health. Definitive source of information on many public health issues, such as secondhand smoke. The IOM also sets the RDAs for vitamins and minerals. (http://www.iom.edu)

Journal of the American Medical Association Leading weekly national medical journal; articles report on latest research and developments. Emailed table of contents and abstracts of articles are free; some free access articles. (http://www.jama.ama-assn.org))

Lab Tests Online Detailed information on clinical lab tests; useful as a quick reference tool and a way to keep up with advances in testing. (http://www.labtestsonline.org)

Mayo Clinic Comprehensive, accurate guides to conditions, drugs, tests and procedures, and more. Patient-oriented but also valuable for professionals. (http://www.mayoclinic.com)

MediLexicon World's largest online database of pharmaceutical and medical abbreviations—more than 230,000 entries. Updated daily to include new acronyms and abbreviations. (http://www.medilexicon.com)

Medline Plus Authoritative information from National Library of Medicine, the National Institutes of Health (NIH), and other government agencies and health-related organizations. Easy access to medical journal articles along with extensive information about drugs, an illustrated medical encyclopedia, and latest health news. (http://www.medlineplus.gov)

Medscape Professional health care content, including review articles, journal commentary, expert columns, patient education articles, hundreds of online CME activities, and conference coverage. Part of WebMD.com. (http://www.medscape.com)

MerckMedicus.com Excellent one-stop source for breaking medical news and a wide variety of online learning resources. Sponsored by Merck, a major pharmceutical company and publisher of the most widely read medical text in the world, *The Merck Manual of Diagnosis and Therapy.* (http://www.merckmedicus.com)

National Cancer Institute Definitive source of accurate information on cancer diagnosis, treatment, and research from the National Institutes of Health. (http://www.cancer.gov)

National Center for Complementary and Alternative Medicine Lead government agency for information on the diverse medical and health care systems, practices, and products that are not generally considered part of conventional medicine. Reliable, accurate information. (http://www.nccam.nih.gov)

National Comprehensive Cancer Network (NCCN) A not-for-profit alliance of 21 of the world's leading cancer centers, NCCN provides evidence-based cancer information and CME programs. (http://www.nccn.org))

National Heart, Lung and Blood Institute Clinical practice guidelines, CME, links, and more from an authoritative source. (http://www.nhlbi.nih.gov)

National Institutes of Health The starting point for reaching any of the 27 institutes and centers that make up the NIH. (http://www.nih.gov)

Natural Medicines Comprehensive Database This Web site is the scientific gold standard for evidence-based, clinical information on natural medicines. Some features are subscriber-only. (http://www.naturaldatabase.com)

New England Journal of Medicine One of the most important medical journals in the world; published weekly. E-mailed table of contents and article abstracts are free; some content is also free. (http://www.content.nejm.org)

NOAH: New York Online Access to Health Access to high-quality, unbiased consumer health information in English and Spanish. A good choice for patients as a portal to further information. (http://www.noah-health.org)

Office of Dietary Supplements Evidence-based, accurate information on dietary supplements (vitamins, minerals, herbs, and others) from the NIH. (http://www.ods.od.nih.gov)

OncoLink Comprehensive information about specific types of cancer, updates on cancer treatments and news about research advances. Sponsored by the Abramson Cancer Center at the University of Pennsylvania. (http://www.oncolink.com)

PubMed A database of more than 19 million citations for biomedical articles from MEDLINE and life science journals. The basic starting point for any health care research project. (http://www.ncbi.nlm.nih.gov/sites/entrez)

SearchMedica: Professional Medical Search Medical search engine that deliver only the most clinically reputable content intended for practicing medical clinicians. A good way to avoid inaccurate or misleading online health sites. (http://www.searchmedica.com)

Theheart.org Professionally oriented Web site on caring for people with disorders of the heart and circulation, and on preventing such disorders. Content is produced by Medscape/WebMD. (http://www.theheart.org)

U.S. Food and Drug Administration (FDA) Starting point for areas the FDA regulates, including drugs, vaccines, medical devices, and the food supply. (http://www.fda.gov)

WebMD Credible and in-depth medical news, features, reference material, and online community programs. Excellent starting point for professional and patient information. (http://www.webmd.com)

Womenshealth.gov Solid information from the Office on Women's Health, part of the U.S. Department of Health and Human Services. (http://www.womenshealth.gov)

Index